"Franne McNeal is a force of nature. This book is fueled by her tremendous, generous energy and full of courageous, useful insights that can truly help you transform yourself and your business. Franne understands that significance is created from the inside out."

—**Margie Strosser,** *MFA,*
Award-winning Television Producer and Story Consultant

"I would definitely recommend the book to women who need encouragement and might feel "stuck" in their lives. I love that it is relevant to women of all ages and who find themselves at different places within the broad spectrum of personal and professional situations."

—**Lynn Zuckerman Gray,** *Founder and Chief Executive Officer,*
Campus Scout, LLC

"Whether you are an entrepreneur or someone going through a career change, you will gain encouragement and inspiration from this book. Franne has used her personal stories to remind us that we are, indeed, Significant! We have the power to triumph after major setbacks."

—**Daisy Wright,** *Founder and Lead Career*
Strategist, The Wright Career Solution

"Franne reminds us that the doors to happiness and fulfillment in our lives are often unlocked by small actions based on right relationships with one another. Read and re-read this book to find the significance in the stories of your life."

—**Susan L. Prosapio,** *former Executive Director,*
Greater River Arts Association

"The best part of this book is that Franne proves that messages that inspire can be simple and straight-forward."

—**Eve Thompson,** *Country Representative,*
Democratic Republic of Congo, National Democratic Institute for International Affairs

Significant!

From Frustrated
to FranneTastic

Significant!

From Frustrated
to FranneTastic

*Inspirational stories for
the entrepreneurial woman*

by Franne McNeal, MBA
Significant Business Results Coach

This material is copyrighted, ©2013, by Franne McNeal, MBA, Significant Business Results Coach. No part, in whole or in part, may be reproduced by any process, or any other exclusive right exercised, without the permission of the publisher, Significant Business Results, LLC.

The cover design and illustrations are copyrighted, ©2013, by Everaldo Gallimore, Creative Director, Gallimore Design. No part, in whole or in part, may be reproduced by any process, or any other exclusive right exercised, without the permission of Gallimore Design.

Fourth Printing, June 2015

Published by:
Significant Business Results, LLC
P. O. Box 807
Bryn Mawr, PA 19010
www.SignificantBusinessResults.com
Publisher@SignificantBusinessResults.com
215-552-8719

Disclaimer and/or Legal Notices:
While every attempt has been made to verify information provided in this book, neither the author nor the publisher assumes any responsibility for any errors, omissions, or inaccuracies.

Any slights of people or organizations are unintentional. If advice concerning legal or related matters is needed, the services of a qualified professional should be sought. This book is not intended as a source of legal or accounting advice. You should be aware of any laws which govern business transactions or other business practices in your state or province.

Printed in the United States of America
ISBN-13: 978-0-9791643-6-1

DEDICATION

I dedicate this book to my grandfather

George Edward McNeal, Sr.

*whose creativity and perseverance in his small businesses
inspired my life journey and this book.*

TABLE OF CONTENTS

TABLE OF CONTENTS

(continued)

FOREWORD

Decisions, decisions, decisions! All women face them, but we aren't always sure how to choose wisely or manage life's challenges. In the course of negotiating promotions, startups, setbacks, career changes, finances, partnerships and friendships, we may find ourselves paralyzed by fear, indecision and doubt. But women today want to step up, lean in, and create change! And as we demand ever more of our personal lives and careers, we need a savvy mentor to show us how to make choices that not only bring success, but also harmonize with who we really are – and who we want to be. Franne McNeal is that mentor.

I have been Franne's friend and colleague for many years, and I have seen her overcome the kind of life challenges that would defeat a lesser person. Her undeniably positive outlook has been heartening to me, and will surely encourage readers of this unique book. *Whether you are an entrepreneur or not, you will recognize a bit of yourself in Franne's stories, and you will profit from her message of conscious living and resilience.*

In *Significant!* Franne offers the intimate testimony of the determination, challenges and triumph of a black businesswoman in America, a point of view which has been unrepresented in print until now. *Significant!* shows how to strategize, cultivate and connect with the same kind of soulful wisdom and creative engagement found in the classic personal development book "The Artist's Way" by Julia Cameron.

Franne teaches us how to move beyond pain and creative constriction, how to recognize and resolve fear, and how to remove emotional scar tissue and attain confidence. She is a master of evocative storytelling, and her experiences in bootstrapping and engaging passionately with other people offer timely lessons to all women, whether they are students, Fortune 500 executives, or kitchen-counter entrepreneurs. Franne emphasizes the importance of defining yourself on your own terms, recognizing the sweet spot of opportunity, and dedicating your wholehearted efforts to self, enterprise, family and community. With quiet humor, illustrative examples, and the workbook-style questions at the end of every chapter, Franne encourages her reader to mine her own personal stories, to discover her most authentic self, and to chart her personal pathway to success.

Years ago, I lacked a map for my career path. I reinvented myself many times, working in the publishing, marketing, non-profit and education industries, and I often yearned for a friendly woman mentor who could guide my ambitious career dreams. Fortunately for me, in 2006, that mentor appeared in my life in the form of Franne McNeal. With good humor and patience, she took me and several of my friends under her protective wing, and she taught us the secrets of building a business from seed to market. We shared many stories, laughs, and even tears, and real successes sprouted from the seeds Franne sewed in our hearts and minds. I am so glad that Franne's mentoring is finally available to a wider circle of women!

As someone already familiar with Franne's coaching techniques, I found that this book has challenged me to open up still further, to explore with greater depth the meaning of the events of my life and, in so doing, to learn to mentor myself effectively. It will do the same for you.

Franne is special: she's an expert facilitator, all-star small business coach, and a trailblazer. But she is also a down-to-earth woman who has dedicated her life to helping other women. Everybody can connect with Franne's stories, and the pearls of wisdom she dispenses in this powerful little book are those of a seasoned pro who is able to speak to the reader like a true friend. Franne advises us not just to think outside the box, but to burn the box! Ultimately, she asks us to find success in business and life by living authentically. *Significant!* is a book to be shared with friends, and revisited many, many times.

Warmly,
Monica O. Montgomery
Millennial Strategist, Museum Administrator, Creative Connector

PREFACE

Everybody has to end up somewhere. That's life! Things happen or they don't, and we reactively turn left or veer right. Our choices combine with and flow from events that are beyond our control to create the sum total of our lives. And in an ever-changing world, it may seem as if the things we *decide* to do could never be truly meaningful in the face of all that just simply *happens*. Our life stories start to feel like collections of random events, notes scribbled on a calendar. We grow up, go to school, choose a career, love whomever we love, and learn as much as we can along the way.

That's one way to look at it. Another way is to consider that everything that happens to us is useful and integral to our lives and the choices we make. We can see our personal stories, both the life events we choose and the ones we don't, as rich and dynamic, a beautiful garden full of color and character derived from a multiplicity of sources. Our actions are part of a great mosaic to which we can consciously add a piece every day.

After decades of working for myself and others in the business world, I've learned that almost everything is negotiable. I've found myself in situations where I felt stuck, uninspired, unappreciated. I say "found myself" intentionally; because it's from those moments when things just *happen* to us that we can mine some of our greatest lessons, and it's in those moments of frustration when we are closest to liberty and to acknowledging that we alone have the power to consciously create our lives. It's in those difficult moments when we choose who we will become.

This book is meant to show you how to negotiate that process, no matter where you're starting from, and no matter where you want to go. As a business coach, I've helped new entrepreneurs create thriving operations that solve a specific problem, and I've helped established business owners make millions of dollars by pushing them to do what they do in the best, most effective way possible. Then in 2013, I was the lead facilitator of a New York City-based "Lean In" group, the largest in the world at that time, and there I quickly saw the power of story to reveal each person's true self and motive force.

I am a person who is so private about her personal life that I refer to myself as "The Armadillo"! You know, that animal with the hard protective shell that curls into a ball when threatened? So for me it has been a life-changing decision to gather these personal stories to share with you. For me, writing this book has been a sometimes grueling but always interesting process of remembering, exploring, and searching for meaning in the details of my own life story, including my 30 years as a successful woman in business.

In this book, I challenge you to do what I have done, and I will help you through the process. You'll learn how to cull your own life story to generate the energy you need to get started, and you'll learn how to convert that energy into meaningful opportunities. You'll find out how to seek the support you will inevitably need along the way, and you'll also discover ways to start appreciating your life more, right now. The goal? To help you be as significant as you can be.

This book is organized into five sections that reflect five main themes. I introduce each section with a fable or folktale, followed by a brief discussion of how the lesson of that fable relates to the very personal stories I am going to tell you. I hope that you are entertained by the stories, but most of all I hope that you are inspired by them to see that the success of your own ventures depends upon the clarity with which you understand your true self and your ability to continually make smart edits and additions in the unfolding story of your own life. I hope that my stories will show you that being significant isn't about power or high net worth, although significant people often do attain those things. Rather, significance is about recognizing your own intrinsic value, communicating it to others, and using it to attract support so that you can create the life and career that you want.

Significant! is a workbook that requires your active participation. The questions that follow each chapter are meant to help you take a step back from my story in order for you to gain deeper insight into your own. When you are digging into your own stories, you are both protagonist and narrator, you are both the star of the show and the audience. I can assure you that this kind of fluid engagement can be hard work! And although it may feel strange at first as most new things do, you'll find out eventually that if you respond to my questions sincerely, you'll learn a lot about yourself and your goals. More importantly, you will learn about the beliefs you have which you might not be completely conscious of without a little intentional digging in the fertile garden of your life. It can be fun to be the subject of an interview! Indulge, spend time, and enjoy learning about yourself, and you will have a harvest of new insights and personal growth.

This process is effective if you do it alone, but I really encourage you to find a good friend or a group of supportive people who can act as your sounding board and push your answers and responses. Don't feel compelled to stay within the questions I ask you, either. Feel free to go where the "interview" takes you; ask follow-up questions that take you even deeper. The discussions that evolve from group inquiry can be surprisingly empowering and often have lasting positive effects.

Do you want more feedback? Register and become part of the **www. SignificantYou.com** online community so you can receive the following benefits:

▶ Connect with like-minded people

- ▶ Find and access useful resources
- ▶ Download additional tools
- ▶ Participate in virtual events
- ▶ Organize and attend local and regional events
- ▶ Share your stories of significance
- ▶ Meet the author of *Significant!*

Now, get to work and start claiming your significance! Thank you for joining me on this wonderful journey.

Significantly yours in success,

Franne McNeal, MBA
Significant Business Results Coach
Franne@SignificantYou.com
www.SignificantYou.com

ACKNOWLEDGEMENTS

First and foremost, thank you to my parents Dr. George Edward McNeal, Jr. and Dr. Lynnette Hammond McNeal, and to my sisters Nancy, Jacqueline, and Marilyn for encouraging and supporting my entrepreneurial spirit.

I owe a great debt to my community of mentors, clients, students, coaches, professors, and friends who have encouraged me to share my confidence and competence as an entrepreneur and Significant Business Results Coach. In particular, thanks go to my book review team: Angelica Aguirre, Debra Y. Boler, Mika Bulmash, Christina Cruz, Suzanne Curran, Tanya Dotson, Keith Ellison, Renetta English, Sandra G. Ford, Dana-René Gaines, Lynn Z. Gray, Ilene Hass, Cheresse Harris, Deloris Henderson, Jacqueline Hill, Carla F. Holland, Sandy Holtzman, Theresa Hummel-Krallinger, Cathy Imburgia, Leia Jackson, Jennifer Jones, Norma Long, Obioma Martin, Edwina McNeal, Jimmy Mac McNeal, Phyllis McNeal, Tanya T. Morris, Mrs. Evelyn Mosby, Wanda F. Muhammad, Wender Ozuna, Parisnicole Payton, Susan L. Prosapio, Tracey Ragsdale-Mabrey, Charles Reaves, Ron Story, Margie Strosser, John L. Thompson, LaSonya Thompson, Yvonne Tucker, Chanelle Washington, Helena Boller Watts, Agnieszka Wilk, April M. Williams, Debbie Scott Williams, Jo-Ann Williams, Barrington Wright, and Daisy Wright.

Thank you to photographer Alan Bogusky, photographer Galo Delgado, hair stylist Aletha Green Mullen, and Creative Director Everaldo Gallimore for making me look Significant!

Thank you to my book consultation team who brought their insights to my original idea and book outline: Dr. Margaret Brito, Margie Smith Holt, Russell D. James, Marilyn M. McNeal, Monica O. Montgomery, and Natalie Nevares. Gratitude also to the publicity consultation team, Angela J. Carter, Tené Croom and Diane I. Daniels, who gave me early feedback about how much work I had left to do!

Thank you to the people whose lives, heart and wisdom combined with mine to form some of the stories that I tell in this book, including Cindy Harrington, Benayah Johnson, Brandon Johnson, Kris Johnson, Stephanie Johnson, Rebecca Kruer, Bernie McGinley, Donald Patterson Jr., Susy Prosapio, Gabriel Ralph, Julia Gusftason Wagner, Chrissy Wiley, Susan O. Wood and Shushi Yoshinaga.

And, lastly, thank you to my editor Dorothy Potter Snyder.

The Stag at the River (Aesop)

A stag had grown thirsty and went to a spring in order to drink some water. When he saw the reflection of his body in the water, he disparaged the slenderness of his legs but reveled in the shape and size of his horns. All of a sudden, some hunters appeared and began to chase him. As the stag ran along the meadow, he outdistanced his pursuers and beat them to the marsh by the river. Without thinking about what he was doing, the stag plunged into the brush, and his horns became entangled in the overhanging branches so that he was captured by the hunters. The stag groaned and said, 'Woe is me, wretched creature that I am! The thing that I disparaged could have saved me, while I have been destroyed by the very thing I boasted about.'

Moral: The most valuable things are often disregarded.

GET GOING!

"If you can't fly, run. If you can't run, walk. If you can't walk, crawl. But by all means, keep moving." —Martin Luther King, Jr.

Before we start, I'd like to thank you for joining me on this journey. Let's take a moment to set the stage a bit. Just ahead, you'll read stories from my life about specific moments when I've met challenges and opportunities head-on, from the formative years of childhood to some serious obstacles I met in adulthood. In each story, I'll share with you my take-away from that particular situation. I can tell you briefly that the focus is decidedly motivational.

The stories in this first section are about getting up, getting out, and getting going! However, I want to encourage you from this moment on to take ownership of these stories, and to use them as a mirror into your own life. What challenges are you facing and how are you handling them? What talents do you possess and how are you using them?

Sharp focus and self-inquiry are the beginning steps to creating the energy and momentum that you need for what you want to achieve. The stag in Aesop's tale failed to grasp what his strongest feature was, and the result was fatal! In this first section of the book, our aim is to avoid making the same mistake.

As you use this book, feel free to pause in the middle of a story if you need to, bookmark the page, and come back later. It's important to take the time to really consider what *your* story is, who *you* really are, and what possibilities are available to *you*, right now. How do your stories match mine? And how are they different?

My stories will always be available here in this book for you to refer back to. But your own opportunities and insights are fleeting, so grasp them while you can! Patience is a key part of this journey we are taking together, so take time to ponder and answer the questions I ask you at the end of each section. By writing your own story, you will be reflecting an image back at yourself that will slowly become clearer and sharper, helping you to arrive at new insights and to see how Significant you truly are.

1

Offer of a Bike

"Mankind's greatest gift, also its greatest curse,
is that we have free choice. We can make our choices
built from love or from fear." —Elisabeth Kubler-Ross

Like most teenagers in their senior year of high school, I was experiencing rites of passage:among those rites of youth was learning to drive and getting a car. My parents saw to it that my sisters and I received a first-class education, and for me that meant an excellent private girl's school on the Main Line of Philadelphia. So believe me, the cars that some of my classmates started driving to school weren't old jalopies! Shiny new BMWs and Mercedes started popping up in the school parking lot, and sprinkled in among those luxury brands were the more understated but still impressive Volvos and Volkswagens. Well, I was growing up too, and I decided that I needed a more adult image! So I approached myparents about buying me a car.

My mother raised an eyebrow at my request, and her answer was rapid and no-nonsense: "How about a bike?" But I protested. A bicycle wasn't at all what I had in mind! "*All* my classmates are getting cars", I exaggerated wildly with the outraged conviction that I felt as a teenager. "Why can't I have a car, too?" My mother pointed out the obvious fact that we lived very close to the school, so close in fact that I could walk there if I wanted to. But the second thing she said that day has stuck with me forever: "Wrappings can be trappings," she said with characteristic economy of expression.

"School is about what you do when you're there, Frances, not how you get there."

I took the bike.

My mother's offer of a bike reflected her core value that functionality -- e.g. learning and getting good grades -- is more important than appearances. This is one of those "metronomic" themes that I have returned to over and over again throughout my life to measure what I thought I wanted against what was the most functional and practical choice for the time and place.

I can think of many times when I have had a big choice to make that my mother's offer of a bike popped into my mind before I made my decision. Would I make my parents pay extra for a single dorm room in college, or would I be content with a double? *It's not where you sleep that counts, Frances, it's where you are when you're awake!* When I got my first corporate job, would I live at home with parents or buy my own apartment? *See above.* When I became an entrepreneur, would I buy a car or take public transportation? *It's not the vehicle you get there in, Frances, it's the work you do when you arrive!* Was I going to take on an intern to help me in my business, or was I going to hire a freelancer? *It's not who's doing the work, Frances, it's how!* Valuing purpose over appearance is how my mother taught me to evaluate my choices and make wise decisions.

In the personal stories that I am going to tell you in this book, I will be talking a lot about choice. Because *choice is something that everyone without exception possesses in every moment.* There are always choices to be made, and sometimes your smallest choices can be the biggest game-changers! Even making the choice to make no choice at all results in consequences that can impact your life, usually in negative ways!

Life is making choices, but learning how to make wise choices is not a simple task. My mother was wise to deny me the indulgence of the new car that some of my peers were getting, even though she and my father could definitely have afforded to give in to my request. Instead, she taught me to ask the right questions when choosing between one thing and another: Is it necessary? Is it functional? Does it match who I'm with, where I am, and, perhaps most important of all, does it match who I am?

The memory of the shiny new Schwinn bike that my parents bought me back in high school is a symbol of the questions that I ask myself whenever an important decision looms. Those questions are a ruler that I use to take the measure of any scheme, purchase, or investment of my time.

Of course, we all make poor decisions sometimes, and I promise that you'll hear about some of the poor choices I've made later on in this book! But as you acknowledge that you actually have choices, and develop an ethic for making decisions based on your authentic core values, you will get smarter about how you choose. Eventually, you will be able to trace the history and growth of your own wisdom through a careful accounting of your accomplishments, which will be in the history of your life like the marks on a doorframe made by a parent to track the growth of a beloved child.

Becoming a good decision-maker is not about being right all the time; it's about knowing where you aregoing and why you are going there. Avoid getting entangled in the trappings of life, and stay focused on your core purpose.

*　*　*　*　*

"I must judge, I must choose, I must spurn, purely for myself.
For myself, alone." —Hermann Hesse

Discussion Questions

Take action. Write down your responses. Share with a friend.

1. When have you wanted something that someone else had, just because it seemed to be significant as a rite of passage? What did the object mean to you?

2. What are your core values around functionality, practicality and purpose? What or who influenced your attitudes and beliefs about those core values?

3. How do you know whether there is a choice to be made? What core values do you depend on to *guide* your choices? How do you *evaluate* the results of your choices or decisions based on your authentic core value?

4. When has a small choice or decision been a game-changer for you?

5. When has making *no* choice or decision about something had a large impact or been a turning point for you?

6. How do you react when you've made a poor choice? How do you stay focused on your core purpose?

2

Carpe Diem!

"With every experience, you alone are painting your own canvas, thought by thought, choice by choice." —Oprah Winfrey

When I was admitted to Princeton at age 16, women were a relatively new part of the student population. I felt like I was participating in history, and I had plans to conquer the world. Wherever I sat was the seat of all possibility.

But in that atmosphere of tradition, privilege, and intellectual rigor, I learned a few things very quickly. First, I learned that just because I was smart didn't mean that I was going to get heard, and I experienced what it was like to be compartmentalized. People saw me as a "black student", a "female student", or a "young student" instead of what I felt like, which was a smart and energetic member of a dynamic peer group. Like the stag in Aesop's fable, I was looking at my reflection, trying to discern my best characteristics. But the other people around me saw something completely different and infinitely less subtle!

Some of my friends at Princeton had similar experiences of alienation, and they found solace in sports, college social life, or in becoming bookworms. But just locking my dorm room and getting lost in a textbook didn't feel like conquering the world to me! I wanted to *engage*. So I ran for student government, participated in the Women's Center, signed up for internships and took a part-time job. Then something really interesting happened.

My part-time job was a research position in a stock broker's office just off campus. One thing that I noticed right away was that the people in that office made money by making connections: networking was more than half of their job. Then one day, I overheard one of the partners talking about what a pain it was to organize networking parties.

Cue the cartoon light bulb.

I'd done party planning in high school, and because I had been so active on campus, I knew lots of students who wanted a way to make money that didn't include working in the cafeteria. I thought that I could organize the parties, so I seized that moment and proposed just that to the partner I'd overheard complaining. He agreed, and it was one of those "click" moments where everything just falls into place.

Looking back, I realize that the challenges and obstacles I faced were actually gifts. I derived tons of energy from the thrill of being at the crossroads of history and potential -- remember, women had only been at Princeton for a little over a decade! Being on the cutting edge of history only sharpened my saw. The awareness of who I was in the context of history gave me the confidence to reach out to form real relationships with people who weren't like me,the drive to assert myself, take risks, and speak up. In the case of the stockbroker's parties, speaking up led to a real opportunity for me and my peers.

I was a junior in college running my first small business with a payroll and employees. Suddenly those distinctions of gender, age and race mattered less because I was providing jobs to my peers and a service to my employer. And I was having so much fun!

I own many more businesses in my life, and all of them involved the same basic process that I discovered in college. Take note of what you've got, and who you really are; identify opportunities; and extend yourself fearlessly to make the connection.

* * * * *

"Your attitude, not your aptitude, will determine your altitude."
—*Zig Ziglar*

Discussion Questions

Take action. Write down your responses. Share with a friend.

1. When did you not feel "seen" by others? What did you do about it?

2. What are three skills you have that you believe are valuable?

3. When is the last time you took a chance based on the skills you've identified? Did it pay off?

4. What is your dream opportunity? Feel free to be as pie-in-the-sky or creative as you want. Provide details.

5. What obstacles are between you and that opportunity?

6. Can you think of any "hidden" resources around you—friends, possessions, or knowledge?

7. Imagine that your skills, an opportunity and resources combine to inspire a business. What is that business? Describe it in detail.

3

Member of the Club?

"No one can make you feel inferior without your consent." —*Eleanor Roosevelt*

I have never been a shrinking violet. I was fortunate to grow up with parents who instilled in me and my sisters a strong sense of self-worth and confidence, and so my natural style is more full-court press than a strong defensive game. That said, even a bullish character like me had to learn that sometimes the best way to lead is to get out of the way.

In my junior year at Princeton, I was elected the first black woman President of Cloister Inn, one of Princeton University's most prestigious eating clubs. The Cloister Inn is a marvelous neo-gothic structure founded in 1912. It claims numerous well-known public figures in its membership rolls, and it has even appeared in a few movies and famous books! The Cloister Inn and the other private eating clubs on "The Street" are a venerable part of Princeton tradition.

When I entered Princeton, it had only been admitting women as undergraduates for nine years, and women like me were still pioneering the corridors of influence and power. Opinions about co-education were divided among male alumni whose experience of Princeton was as a single sex institution.

So it was in this atmosphere that I was elected the President of Cloister Inn by my peers. It was a huge honor and big responsibility that I was

thrilled to take on. It gave me a chance to flex my leadership muscles in an arena that included not only fellow students, but also important alumni. I took the lead in Club events, assuming personal responsibility for their success and thriving under the pressure. But then something happened that taught me that it's not enough to be the leader; others have to see you as a leader, too.

Every May on Reunion Weekend, Princeton fills up with nearly twenty-thousand alumni and their families. For alumni, it's a way to reconnect with classmates, and see how campus life has changed. For the school, the events of Reunion Weekend provide a celebratory atmosphere to reconnect alumni to the school and encourage their financial support of its programs so that future students can also experience a world-class education. There are talks, community service projects, picnics, parties, dancing and, of course, marching in the One and Only "P-rade"! The reunion classes march for the spectators with their banners held high; and the eldest marchers, the "Old Guard", always draw the loudest cheers from spectators as they amble past in their hats and blazers to the spirited sounds of the marching band.

Because reunion weekend is such a big party, all the social organizations and eating clubs hold events, and since I was President of Cloister Inn, I took the lead in organizing an evening party that involved hors d'oeuvres and, of course, beer. Lots of beer. The mood was festive, with the outgoing seniors interacting with the older alums, talking and comparing notes. And did I mention that there was lots of beer? People drank, and some people drank more than others. Some people got quite drunk.

I became aware of an alumnus who was starting to make a bit of a scene. It is important to note that he was white, male and a good bit my senior. I knew that as President it was my role to be diplomatic and deal with the situation, so I said firmly but politely. "Excuse me, Sir, do you need help?" He ignored me, and kept talking to his buddy, and may have even raised his voice a little more. "Would you like to sit down?" I said, hoping to help him decide that it might be time for him to either just relax, or to go home. "Who are *you*?" he retorted, at an even louder volume. "I'm the President of this club," I replied, managing to step on his toe and knock his beer over in the process. "How *dare* you talk to me that way!" he snarled. I was a bit confused, wondering what was offensive about identifying myself as the President of the club! The alumnus muttered something to his friend, and I can't really tell you what he said, but the body language was highly dismissive. Not registering my "dismissal", I piped up a bit louder, "Excuse me, Sir, do you need help?"

That did it. The alumnus exploded with rage. "Who do you think you are telling me what to do? I've been a member of this club for longer than you've been alive! Who are you to tell me what to do?" As his voice got louder and beer sloshed out of his glass, he started getting a bit too close to me for comfort. I felt as if I had stepped on a grenade. I breathed, stepped back, and shifted my weight.

I quickly realized that as a young black woman, President or not, I was not going to get anywhere with this man. So I called out to Trevor, the boyfriend of one of my friends. Trevor was white, 6 feet tall, and dressed in chinos and an Oxford cloth shirt; in other words, the perfect preppie. Trevor strode over to conciliate the drunk alumnus – and I stepped away. Within seconds, the incident was over.

I was taken aback at first by the man's disrespectful way of addressing me, but only for a moment. I realized instantly that in the game of perception, this alumnus truly didn't see me as embodying a Princeton eating club President, and so he questioned it. Part of leadership is perceiving what others expect to see in their leader and, to some degree, making small adjustments to help them see the kind of person that they feel best able to follow. In this case, I immediately grasped that a white male prep student-type was the only image that this man was going to connect with. I was right. I had made a good adjustment.

The second thing I learned was that most lessons in leadership are learned on the ground, in the moment, when a situation is unfolding before you. As a leader you develop a kind of radar around other people and, in the same way that a pilot adjusts the flaps on the wings to reduce the wind drag on his aircraft, you learn to adjust your own "wings" depending on the "weather" of whatever situation you're in. You may need to tilt left, or tilt right; sometimes you need to fly a straight course. Deciding how to react to challenges to your authority is a skill that requires lots of practice, and your success in learning that skill will determine to a large degree the kind of results you get as a leader.

I am proud of this story because I was very young when it happened, and I did the right thing instinctively; furthermore, I got the results I wanted, which was a successful celebration of Reunion Weekend.

Remember Aesop's stag who ended up getting shot down because he admired his rack of horns more than those swift legs of his that could have saved him? Well, I was proud of my "crowning glory", too! I was proud that I had been elected by my peers to be the President of the Club, and that I was a woman "pioneer" at a traditionally male top Ivy League School. Yes, when I looked at my reflection I was justifiably proud of who I had become! So I could have "flown a straight course" against the rudeness of that drunken alumnus. Instead, my survival instinct clicked on, I "tilted left", and I quickly achieved a positive outcome for everyone at the party.

Sometimes being a good leader means getting out of the way.

*   *   *   *   *

"Not everything that is faced can be changed.
But nothing can be changed until it is faced." —James Baldwin

Discussion Questions

Take action. Write down your responses. Share with a friend.

1. When have you been a "first" or pioneer in an organization or activity? To what degree did you witness debate as to whether "someone like you" should be able to participate in that group or activity?

2. When have you had an opportunity to take a formal leadership role, elected or otherwise? Briefly describe the situation. How did it go?

3. Have you ever been appointed a leader but then felt you were not perceived as a leader? What happened?

4. What did you do to adjust to the perception that you were not the leader? How did your adjustment work for others? How did your adjustment work for you?

5. Did you ever learn a leadership lesson while you were "in the moment"? Describe the moment. What was the leadership lesson?

6. When have you had to "get out of the way" as a leader in order to create a good positive outcome for everyone?

4

Hawaiian Punch

"Not knowing when the dawn will come, I open every door."
—*Emily Dickinson*

I've learned a lot from Hawaiian Punch. It seems strange that I could take life skills away from a sugary fruit drink, but I have.

Growing up, I was the eldest of four sisters. Like many families with kids to keep happy and fed, ours bought in bulk and one of those items was a 48-ounce container of Hawaiian Punch. My mother left it up to me to divide the drink, and each time we got a container, I split it into even 12-ounce portions for my three sisters and myself.

I wasn't above negotiating the Punch terms, either. Maybe one of my sisters wanted to trade a little more punch for something else, or maybe one of them demanded to go first because she always went last. And these weren't just squabbles; they were as intense and reasoned as any boardroom debate. It's a good thing there weren't five of us! I didn't know it then, but by being the Hawaiian Punch disbursement officer, I was learning to manage resources, and to navigate the yes/no spectrum.

I took an early interest in computers, and by the time I was at the University of Pittsburgh studying for my MBA, I was also teaching non-credit courses in computer technology. I enjoyed helping people learn, and I wondered if providing access to new technology was a way for me to create income for myself. I did some research, and I found an internship with a computer training company.

During the interview, the hiring manager said she was reluctant to offer me the position because she thought I'd be a future competitor. All those Hawaiian Punch instincts kicked into action almost immediately! I imagined myself jostling for space with my three sisters, and instead of letting the HR manager's "no" dampen my enthusiasm, I used it to strengthen my resolve. I took her rejection as a suggestion.

I knew that this company was in the running for a City of Pittsburgh contract to teach employees computer technology, and I decided to compete for the contract right then and there, exactly as the hiring manager had suggested!

I answered the City's proposal request, and had a long series of meetings with city officials that went something like this --

City Official: Can you do this?

Me: Yes.

City Official: Do you want to do this?

Me: Yes.

City Official: Are you sure?

Me: Absolutely.

I won the contract.

It was a massive and trying project, but in many ways it was similar to pouring out those 12-ounce cups of Hawaiian Punch. I had to distribute scant resources of time, equipment, and budget very carefully in order to make the project happen.

I didn't have a facility, a car, or computers, and I only had five hundred dollars in the bank. I was able to win and keep a $150,000 municipal contract at age 26 because I knew how to use what I *did* have: specialized content knowledge and skill at conveying it. I had to borrow money to secure computers and a teaching location, and I structured my cash flow so that the people I was employing got paid as I did, and not before. Instead of buying all new textbooks, I made copies and bound them myself. The city paid slowly, so instead of a big full-time staff, I used independent contractors and the advantage of my own youthful energy to keep the ball rolling. In the early years, I knew that one bad review from a client could put the whole business in jeopardy, so I spent time outside my teaching schedule creating relationships.

What did I learn? That the key to handling this potentially overwhelming job was to break the huge task into smaller, "12-ounce" parts. But the even more fundamental lesson, however, was that by being well-acquainted with the woman in the mirror, I knew that I had the skills to do exactly what the job required, and that I had been using those skills my whole life -- ever since the days of Hawaiian Punch!

*   *   *   *   *

"Luck is what happens when preparation meets opportunity."
—*Seneca*

Discussion Questions

Take action. Write down your responses. Share with a friend.

1. Think about the most daunting task you've ever tried to accomplish. What made it so challenging?

2. Did you accomplish it? If so, how? If not, why not?

3. Think of a project that you're working on right now. How can you break it into smaller parts to make it more manageable?

4. Can you remember a time when you believed in yourself and stood up for yourself? Briefly record the event and how it felt.

5. What is something that you think is impossible to do but would like to do? Again, go crazy! Be as creative as you want! Then, write out the first four steps of how to go about doing it.

5

Taking Root

"Courage does not always roar. Sometimes courage
is the little voice at the end of the day that says
I'll try again tomorrow." —Mary Anne Radmacher

I was lying in the hospital staring up at the ceiling. I had suffered a paralyzing stroke and the doctors said it might take months before I had enough muscle strength to start a recovery. In the meantime, they suggested that I just imagine myself moving a toe, or just think about moving a finger. "Just start small," they said, "wiggle, and wait." I thought about gardening, and how good it felt to hold the earth in my fingers, to grow something, *and I wanted to feel that again.* As I was lying in bed, feeling a bit like a dormant seed, one particular event in my life came to mind.

Years earlier, I was a manager at a large financial institution that had offices in Philadelphia and New Jersey. I was given the responsibility of laying off one of our employees, an unfortunate task no manager takes pleasure in. I understood that the employee had to be laid off, but I was not happy about the way it was being done. My superiors were planning to have her come in under the premise that she'd be attending a team meeting; but she was really coming in *before* the team meeting, so that I could tell her she didn't have a job anymore and whisk her away before the rest of the team arrived. I felt sure that there was a better, more humane way that we could handle the situation, especially since this employee had to come from out of state.

When I talked to my boss about it, I was told that I didn't have any options, and that if I pursued the issue further, my own job would be in jeopardy. And in that moment, I felt as mentally immobilized as I would feel physically immobilized years later lying in that hospital bed trying to learn how to move my body again. Even though I chose not to argue with my boss then, I took advantage of the lesson about myself that was inherent in the experience, a lesson that would eventually flower into my next venture: I came face to face with that essential, non-negotiable part of my personality that values honest communication and a straight-forward approach over evasiveness, or an authoritarian stance.

But it took some time until the seed of that self-knowledge took root in me and developed into something that I could articulate and form into a product to share with the world. In that moment, I couldn't conceive of the phrase "significant business results coach," which is what I call myself today. I just knew that clear, respectful communication in business was possible, and that I would not only do it, but teach others how to do it as well.

I knew that I wanted to help people take their ideas, dreams, and skills, and crystallize them into the kind of value that others could recognize and be willing to pay for. I wanted to create "dangerous entrepreneurs" and business owners that had the potential to transform the corporate landscape into one that was more creative and more sincere.

But in that period after my stroke when I was lying helpless in a hospital bed, the energy to achieve that dream of mine seemed so far away! After days and days of lying there and focusing my intention on achieving even the slightest movement, I finally moved a finger. And then another. Eventually, finger by finger, toe by toe, I recovered full motion in my body -- and way ahead of the doctors' schedule, at that!

Just as I worked to regain motion after my stroke and heal my body, I also had some healing to do in my career. Equipped with my dream, I was finally able to leave behind the corporate world of threats and ultimatums and create my own consulting business based on building on positive, sincere relationships.

I have the unshakeable conviction that *anyone* can be a leader and that *anyone* can become great, no matter who they are or where they are starting their journey. Just start small, wiggle, and wait.

*   *   *   *   *

"There are three essentials to leadership:
humility, clarity and courage." —Fuchan Yuan

Discussion Questions

Take action. Write down your responses. Share with a friend.

1. Are there any ways that you feel restricted or inauthentic in the current circumstances of your life? If so, list them here.

2. Can you list what you believe to be your authentic values, the beliefs you hold close?

3. Do you feel like these beliefs are helping you or holding you back?

4. Can you list three personal and/or professional goals that you have right now?

5. Can you list five qualities that you admire about yourself? Can you imagine how those qualities could help you reach your goals?

6. When do you feel most energized? At what time of day? During what activity?

7. What do you think are your best features? Greatest talents? What do you think are your worst features? Can you imagine a positive use for one of your "worst" features?

The Dove and the Ant (Aesop)

An Ant, going to a river to drink, fell in, and was carried along in the stream. A Dove pitied her condition, and threw into the river a small bough, by means of which the Ant gained the shore. The Ant afterward, seeing a man with a fowling-piece aiming at the Dove, stung him in the foot sharply, and made him miss his aim, and so saved the Dove's life.

> **Moral:** Little friends may prove great friends,
> and one good turn deserves another.

EMBRACE OPPORTUNITY

"A pessimist sees the difficulty in every opportunity; an optimist sees the opportunity in every difficulty." —Sir Winston Churchill

Let's take a moment to collect ourselves before continuing our journey. So far, we've seen how it's possible to overcome all kinds of paralysis; emotional, metaphorical, and even physical. And we've also seen that when you're stuck, as I was in a tense work situation, or low on energy, it's imperative to seek out your personal authentic value system and live by it.

We've also seen that when you're aware of all the tremendous resources at your disposal, you notice opportunities much more easily. Once you've taken stock of your character and your resources and you've discovered an opportunity, it's important to choose yourself, negotiate for yourself, and believe in yourself. You must do this even in the face of apparent defeat, like when the City of Pittsburgh purchasing manager said "no" to me just before I decided to pursue the big city contract on my own. Indeed, by communicating her reasons for not hiring me, the purchasing manager became my unwitting ally!

You also have to be able to take opportunity and turn it into real results, real value. But that's only part of the equation. The stories I am going to tell you now are examples –– both good and bad –– of some times in my life when I've found allies just like Aesop's ant and dove, allies who helped me to see my way to new opportunities.

6

The See-Saw Effect

"The question isn't who is going to let me;
it's who is going to stop me." —Ayn Rand

As a little girl, I used to enter the American Family Publishers sweepstakes. I'd sit on the floor of my home in Norristown, PA, carefully follow the entry instructions, address the envelope, and send it off with exact postage required. The thought of Ed McMahon showing up at my door with an oversized check was enticing, but there was also something else at work in me. My parents, both life-long learners, had encouraged me to explore and be curious, and that created in me a sense of freedom and an ability to dream that I wanted to share with others. My secret agenda? I was entering the sweepstakes so I could open a school in my parents' name!

Was I crazy entering that sweepstakes over and over again? Well, I don't think so! When it comes to what you do in life, I believe in the see-saw effect. In other words, what you give is directly related to what you get.

When I was in my mid-twenties, I was working in sales and covering a large territory in Pittsburgh. I think there was a very practical reason that I was given that territory; the company knew that there was a large enough black population that I wouldn't feel isolated, but it was a small enough area that I wouldn't feel overwhelmed.

I began to meet members of the community, and Don Patterson, Jr. was one of those people. Don had grown up in a family of entrepreneurs and had seen first-hand how powerful it is to run your own business. He developed an after-school program that focused on teaching entrepreneurial skills to youth. I was a young black woman creating her own entrepreneurial life, and so Don invited me to speak to his kids.

The speech went well, and afterward, Don created a speakers' circuit that would amplify impact of the speeches like the one I had just given. As the first speaker, Don invited American entrepreneur Earl Graves, Sr., entrepreneur, philanthropist, publisher of Black Enterprise magazine and CEO of his own media company! It was gamble, but it worked, and when Mr. Graves accepted the invitation, a sponsorship from Pepsi covered his speaker's fee. Don invited me to share the dais for that event, and so I was fortunate enough to share the stage with Earl Graves, Sr. -- and I've got the pictures to prove it!

That was certainly a proud moment in my life. I met one of the world's great business leaders, but I also felt a sense of reward from helping to create an inspiring experience for other people, especially young people. It echoed the excitement that I had felt growing up in a home with parents who encouraged me to learn and dream, and it's a feeling is something that I've sought to recreate again and again throughout my career, both as a giver and a receiver of inspiration.

Remembering these experiences, I'm reminded of the motto of my alma mater, Princeton: "In the Nation's Service." I had no idea that that was the spirit that I was developing when I was entering those sweepstakes as a child so that I could build a school in my parents' name, but it was. I had more of an idea of what I was feeling when I helped bring Mr. Graves to speak to young entrepreneurs in Pittsburgh. Today, the commandment to serve is an explicit part of my work as a business coach. Whenever I coach entrepreneurs, I see an opportunity to help them discover their own sense of ability and enthusiasm. When that process is successful, it's a wonderful and dynamic gift. In giving them the tools to discover their freedom on their terms, I find that my own sense of liberty is renewed.

A see-saw is fun, but it takes two people to make it work. Help another person find her way, and you will surely find your own way in the process.

* * * * *

"No man ever listened himself out of a job." —Calvin Coolidge

Discussion Questions

Take action. Write down your responses. Share with a friend.

1. What do you think is a special gift or talent that you have that is worth sharing?

2. When was the last time that you shared that special gift or talent? What happened?

3. When was the last time that someone gave you something? What was it and how did it feel?

4. What's your idea of "service?"

5. Look around you and identify a service that you could provide to someone else that might also help you achieve your goals?

7

Copy Machine

"If you have knowledge, let others light their candles in it."
—*Margaret Fuller*

There was a period of my life when Kinko's copy shop was my second home. It was when I was teaching computer skills for the City of Pittsburgh as a solo contractor. After a full day of work, I'd rest a little, and then head out to the copy shop to make materials for the upcoming week. I would usually arrive between one and three in the morning, and I was there so often that a number of the employees and I were on a first-name basis! I was a regular, and I wasn't alone, either. There were other people that haunted the machines in those late hours, and we "ghosts" came to recognize each other, too. There was a certain type of person that needed to use Kinko's regularly during the graveyard shift, and we were all variations of one another.

One morning around 6 a.m., I overheard someone trying to convince a Kinko's employee to help her adjust a word-processing document. The employee was less than enthusiastic, and refused to help. At the time, I taught people how to use software for a living, and I knew the kind of person who came into work late at night or early in the morning: she needed to get something done, and needed it done now! I could empathize with that, so I decided to lend a hand. It was actually a fairly easy fix and, after we finished, the woman was grateful and impressed. She asked how I knew so much, and I mentioned that I ran a technology consulting business. Well, she gave me that look that people do when they are experiencing a moment of serendipity, and so Aesop's dove had found her ant!

The woman worked at PNC bank, and they needed someone to teach new software to their employees. She passed me the business card of the person in charge of that initiative, a man named Bernie. Of course, I followed through. I won a contract with PNC bank and I approached it with the same work ethic that drove me to Kinko's night after night. As a result of my performance, Bernie referred me to other PNC managers who needed software training.

One internal client was Julia and, over the years, Julia would call on me for my training and consulting services. The PNC contract gave me great experience, I became a better consultant, and I deepened my insight into managing time and relationships. One special contract that Julia connected me to was being the exclusive executive computer coach. I flew all over the country teaching people in senior positions how to use the new technology. It was especially exciting because the job offered me a unique mix of freedom and stability. I also felt like I had found a mentor and partner in Julia. Plus, there was the money: it was a very lucrative contract.

Earlier, I mentioned coincidence, but I really think that night in Kinko's was more an example of synchronicity. I had been working diligently on my city contract, and I had been persistent about making it to Kinko's, even when I would have rather slept. I knew where I wanted to go, and I persisted with such regularity that eventually I was in the right place at the right moment equipped with -- and this is important -- the right spirit of service.

I think it's important to note that I wasn't looking for anything in return when I helped that woman late one night, just as Aesop's dove didn't expect that a mere ant would ever be able to save its life. But I got something anyway! A few minutes of my time given freely led to incredible opportunities, wonderful relationships -- and lots of income.

You really can't know how, when or where your moment will present itself, but it will. So be ready.

* * * * *

"Strive not to be a success, but rather to be of value." —Albert Einstein

Discussion Questions

Take action. Write down your responses. Share with a friend.

1. Think of a time that you worked really hard on something that was important to you. What was driving you?

2. What's your current goal? List three things that you're willing to sacrifice to achieve it.

3. When was the last time you helped a stranger? What did you do?

4. Did you ever get a payback from a generous gesture? What was it?

5. What can you do right now to recreate that dynamic?

8

Taking Notes

"We are not what we know but what we are willing to learn."
—*Mary Catherine Bateson*

The first time I took statistics in college, I didn't exactly set the world on fire; my grade was much lower than I wanted. This was troubling because it didn't meet my personal standards, and because it certainly didn't meet the exacting standards of my parents — both of whom are avid learners and very bright people. However, I signed up for the course again, determined to do better. My statistics instructor the second time around was a young curly-haired grad student who wore sneakers and corduroys, and who taught with contagious enthusiasm. He really *loved* talking about the minutiae of the statistics, and he would even make statistics jokes! Of course, some of my classmates were nonplussed by that style of person; but this teacher's jocular, enthusiastic approach was just what I needed.

Growing up, I noticed that my parents made a practice of always learning. They deliberately sought to teach themselves subjects that would broaden their experience of life. My physician father has taken art classes, and later developed an interest in computers. It isn't unusual to see him amidst a myriad of disassembled computers, operating with scientific precision, taking notes, revising, and starting over when he fails. My mother, also a physician, has studied multiple languages from age 50 until today. In my home, learning wasn't a chore, it was a privilege, and something to be relished and embarked upon with gusto. I grew up that way, and I still love learning.

So when I got that low grade in statistics, it was more than a collegiate mini-drama; it challenged my personal beliefs and sense of rightness. I had never had trouble with academics before, and suddenly learning didn't feel so fun! But attitudes and beliefs are the filters through which we experience our lives, and to a large extent they also determine how much we learn or don't learn. I had to *believe* that I could learn statistics! And that's what was so special about my second instructor; he believed itwas fun, andhis attitude was contagious; I got excited enough about statistics to earn an A in the class.

Today, I focus on understanding basic things like the golden rule — reating others as I want to be treated. And I try to find out why such rules are true. I focus on using my five senses to pick up information from the world around me. I concentrate on the common sense of stillness. I try to be quiet and reflect on the reasons that events happen. I'm always trying to discover new insights, and new ways of seeing. And I take notes. Because if we pay attention to the events in our lives, we can take away more value from them than if we were to simply roll through them without reflection.

I know that I could have simply accepted my initial grade in statistics, and I could have blamed my poor performance in the first class on the teacher. But I chose to remain honest with myself about not meeting my personal standards, remaining confident that I could improve — and I did.

Life really is the greatest classroom—*if*, and only if, we show up, take personal responsibility and show enthusiasm.

And take notes.

* * * * *

"Education costs money. But then so does ignorance." —Sir Claus Moser

Discussion Questions

Take action. Write down your responses. Share with a friend.

1. Briefly write about a time you feel you underperformed. What could you have improved?

2. Write about a time you gave up too soon. Why did you stop? What happened later?

3. Who was the last teacher you had that inspired you? Was it in or out of a classroom? Have you thanked that person?

4. When is the last time that you taught yourself something?

5. Write about a time you pulled victory out of defeat. What happened, and how did you turn the experience around?

6. What are you the most excited to learn about right now? How are you going to go about it? When will you start?

9

System Flaws

"You may be disappointed if you fail,
but you are doomed if you don't try." —Beverly Sills

So much of life is about interdependence and natural alliances. Plants and trees give us oxygen, and we return carbon dioxide to them. The plants then use our exhalations of carbon dioxide to process more oxygen, and so on and so on in an endless virtuous cycle. The planet and all the life on it comprise many interlocking systems that feed and support each other, and one piece of input is turned right around into another piece of output. It's as if all of life is part of one great, cosmic breath.

In the case of human organization, we've developed our own delicate ecosystems that help us accomplish huge tasks that would be otherwise impossible. When it works, it works and great things get done! But sometimes it doesn't work, and systems break down.

In late 2009, I had earned a government contract that allowed me to be a primary vendor rather than a sub-contractor. So I gave another entrepreneur an opportunity to grow his business by being *my* sub-contractor. We agreed that he would pay me a 10% referral fee on his income from this contract for the period of one year. Between paperwork, phone conferences, and general logistics, I had put a tremendous amount of effort into securing this contract, so I was happy to share, but I wanted my piece. After the checks started coming from the government contract, I stopped hearing from the sub-contractor.

Once I was able to catch up with him, he couldn't remember our agreement about the 10% referral fee. For months, I pursued him, but he wasn't willing to honor our agreement. Eventually, I took him to court.

That's an example of a system of interdependence breaking down. I counted on the sub-contractor to respect our agreement, and when he didn't, it forced me to re-organize my resources, spend time negotiating with him and deal with lawyers, and it affected the rest of my business. In hindsight, I could have done more analysis and due diligence before bringing him in on the job. Asking more questions and formalizing our contract through a lawyer or paralegal would have saved me a lot of trouble.

Just as your breath is vital to your life, so is it also vital that you insure that what you give—in energy, resources, and time—will be in some way returned to you. Otherwise, you'll exhaust yourself.

Whenever you're building a system with other people, do your best to encourage transparency and clear communication about expectations and outcomes. But remember, nothing is perfect. The flaws in the structure of a system might not always be apparent, and many can be fixed only once they reach your attention, which is usually when something has gone wrong. When it's time to evaluate a system that involves people, start at respect.

At the root level, my sub-contractor wasn't respecting himself or the value of his word, andthat caused an irreparable disruption of our relationship. If you notice that someone isn't respecting himself or you, be careful. Whatever flows from that point will likely be faultyas well. Respect is a foundation, and it's non-negotiable: it's the breath that we exchange in healthy relationships.

* * * * *

*"A pessimist is one who makes difficulties of his opportunities
and an optimist is one who makes opportunities of his difficulties."*
—*Harry S. Truman*

Discussion Questions

Take action. Write down your responses. Share with a friend.

1. List one situation in which you felt as if you weren't being respected. How did you respond?

2. What "systems" are you currently a part of? How are they functioning? How are they dysfunctioning? Take a moment to analyze what's working and what isn't.

3. List one time when you gave energy to a situation that proved not to be worth it to you. What could you have done differently?

4. Can you think of a system that works really well for you? List three observations about it.

5. Can you think of a time when you extended your trust and it paid off for you? Briefly describe what happened.

The Bundle of Sticks (Aesop)

An old man on the point of death summoned his sons around him to give them some parting advice. He ordered his servants to bring in a bundle of sticks, and said to his eldest son: "Break it." The son strained and strained, but with all his efforts was unable to break the bundle. The other sons also tried, but none of them was successful. "Untie the bundle," said the father, "and each of you take a stick." When they had done so, he called out to them: "Now, break," and each stick was easily broken. "You see my meaning," said their father.

Moral: *Union gives strength.*

FIND SUPPORT

"Generosity lies less in giving much,
than in giving at the right moment." —Jean de la Bruyere

Let's pause again. Isn't it wonderful how what you get out of life is proportionate to what you give? And isn't it equally wonderful the way that positive situations will arise when you do the right thing in the right way enough times?

Helping to bring the wisdom of Earl Graves, Sr. to a broader audience was an awesome experience. And meeting a stranger in the middle of the night at a copy shop––a stranger that ended up helping me develop my career––was a delightful surprise. Giving is its own reward, but sometimes life throws in a wonderful bonus.

Even when things don't work as well as you might want, like when I had to take a business associate to court, there are still valuable nuggets to be taken away. I'll tell you a not-so-secret secret: the biggest part of succeeding after a failure is trying again. The second biggest part is learning from your mistakes and adjusting your behavior accordingly.

Now I understand that I have to put all my energy into the things that are working for me, no matter how small, and to quickly cut loose the things that aren't. Because even when things are working for us, we still need help. As in Aesop's tale of the bundle of sticks, we find that in union comes strength. Let me tell you now about when I've sought others' help -- and found unbreakable strength.

10

Circle of Friends

"The most beautiful discovery true friends make is that they can grow separately without growing apart." —Elizabeth Foley

We don't have unlimited time in our lives, and that makes it important to do what we really want to do each day, the things that make us feel good and that we enjoy. Accomplishments aren't always about a power play or boardroom acrobatics.

One of the most rewarding times of my life was a monthly tea date with a group of international women. We called ourselves the Tea Ladies. We were from Japan, Canada, Australia, and the United States. I'd met the Australian woman, Rebecca, at a church gathering, and I later learned that she was volunteering at a community garden. We started chatting, and made an instant bond over gardening. After we'd known each other for a while, she said she had a group of friends I absolutely had to meet.

Soon after that, I was having monthly dates with my new circle of friends; Becca, Cindy, Gaby, and Shushi. We found tea houses that served formal tea, and even though we didn't wear white muslin gloves, it was a classy affair! I'm usually more introspective and solitary, so it was special to be invited into this circle of women, and to have a group to which I felt I belonged. I relished the adventure of it, the dainty sandwiches and the formality of it. And I cherished the support that we offered each other during our talks. And did we talk! We talked about it all: boyfriends, work, travel, opportunities, and disappointments.

It was such a joy to have friends with whom I could relax. We didn't talk business, and I didn't have to prepare notes. Because we were an international group, my awareness of what was happening around the world expanded, but in a highly personal way, through the eyes of each of these interesting women.

The tea group was a uniquely empowering and transformative experience for me. The members of the group shared a mutual respect and a sense of caring without judgment. We were a community. And sometimes belonging and community come from the most surprising places! A great group of travel companions is invaluable on the road to success; they keep you creative, resourceful, and encouraged.

When I'm working with clients, I always ask if they're working on their business or if their business is working on them. That's not a question just for entrepreneurs or even business people! All of us can and should re-think our approach to life on a regular basis, and consider if we're really making time for what's most important to us. We might not know right away what that thing is, and that's okay.

Build relationships. Be vulnerable. Find strength in supportive relationships. Eventually, you'll have a web of friendly arms to support to you. Life is so much broader than the pursuit of power, and living fully can sometimes be as simple as sharing a cup of tea with a friend.

* * * * *

"The language of friendship is not words but meanings."
—*Henry David Thoreau*

Discussion Questions

Take action. Write down your responses. Share with a friend.

1. How do you describe community?

2. What communities do you belong to? List them and describe the value of each one to you.

3. Describe a situation in which you felt like you shared a set of values with another person. What happened?

4. When was a time when you found strength in your association with other people?

5. In what ways do you feel supported by your different communities or groups of friends now?

6. What support do you offer them?

7. How can your communities help you right now to reach your goals?

11

Always Bring Flowers

"A smile is a curve that sets everything straight." —Phyllis Diller

As society becomes increasingly hyper-connected and information savvy, it can be tough for businesses and leaders to keep up. And while many are chasing results, effectiveness, and a return on investment, the souls of organizations are often overlooked; there is a failure to consider the people themselves, their needs, values, and passions. And that oversight can create very disorienting environments. For example, earlier in my career, I'd reached the level of vice president at a corporation, and I worked hard at my job, but I wasn't fulfilled by it. I felt like I was considered only a manager, one of many agents of the organization, instead of an individual with a story and unique purpose. Basically, I was missing a sense of belonging and being respected, and I went searching for it.

Fortunately, time and place were on my side. I'd heard about a new style of leadership called Appreciative Inquiry. It focuses on re-framing the questions we ask to evince the strengths, experience, and potentials inherent in the members of an organization. It also focuses on cultivating community, by bringing together large, diverse groups of people to examine and enhance what has worked in the past. In short, it's a people-affirming approach that engages change constructively. At the time, there were only a dozen people practicing this approach in the entire nation. One of those people was a woman named Susan, a former executive from

Arthur Anderson, and she was hosting training sessions at her home in Philadelphia.

Even today, I'm not sure what made me do it, but I decided to bring a bunch of beautiful tulips to the first training session. Perhaps that the sessions were in her home changed the timbre of the moment. This was a woman who'd been at a top position in one of the biggest accounting firms in the United States—she'd seen all of the power moves, but my flowers weren't received as one of them. She was gracious and accepting; she even presented the tulips to the rest of the group.

Over the next few months, I learned the intensive practice of Appreciative Inquiry. For the first time in a long time, I felt like I was part of a team, like I was connected to a group of people through a common vision and goal. In this case, the goal was to be a more effective group of organizational development consultants and leaders. The spirit of the group was collaborative and sincerely curious. Without a doubt, this atmosphere developed because Susan fostered it.

During that time, I gained skills that I still use today. And I also began relationships that led to tremendous professional opportunities. I believe that this was so because I brought my whole self to a receptive and inclusive group. I had no way of knowing that this would be the case before I went to Susan's house, but I decided to make the small gesture of bringing a gift, and it created a tone that lasted.

We can all do this in one way or another. Whatever we have that blooms, or that lightens the room, we can offer it to the group. We can cultivate meaningful connections. And out of those bonds of sincere appreciation, beautiful new things can grow.

Whenever you go somewhere new, always bring flowers.

* * * * *

"No act of kindness, no matter how small, is ever wasted." —Aesop

Discussion Questions

Take action. Write down your responses. Share with a friend.

1. What is appreciation to you? What does it look and feel like?

2. When was the last time you showed appreciation for another person's talents? How did you do it?

3. When was a time when you were praised for a talent or action? How did it feel?

4. What gift do you have that you haven't shared with anyone yet? What do you think might happen if you did share that gift?

5. Who are the people you feel best around?

6. What can you do right now to make those people in your life feel appreciated?

12

Open the Way

"Life is what we make it, always has been, always will be."
—*Grandma Moses*

One of the things I get most excited about is when I'm invited to serve as a facilitator, because it's my opportunity to direct people in taking specific action that will move everyone forward.

Facilitating is all about leading people to their own realizations and opening them up to the possibility and value of making small changes. I'm often invited by organizations to create and lead a discussion in order to solve a specific problem. That's facilitation at the most basic level, and it's a very powerful tool.

One interesting experience I had was when I was invited to help solve a dilemma for a children's hospital in Philadelphia. The hospital had been designated as a magnet hospital, which is a prestigious honor. The managers were proud of that status and wanted to protect it, but they faced a serious issue; some of the nursing staff felt as if they weren't being given due credit, even though they were a major element of the hospital's success. They felt that while it might be the doctor who delivered the news that someone was going to lose a child, it was the nurses who managed the care of the dying patient and the communication with the grieving family. Of course, the hospital viewed the knowledge and experience of the nurses as an asset and needed them and their dedication. But there was a conflict between the hospital's magnet status and the resentment felt by key staff.

My task was to help the nurses face that conflict and move forward in a positive direction. I was part of a team of consultants sharing the 4-D process of "Discover, Dream, Design and Deliver" that involved all three shifts of nurses. The entire nursing department had an opportunity to be part of defining who they would be within the organization, and take ownership of their importantrole on the hospital team.

So I facilitated a series of one-on-one and group interviews among the diverse groups of nurses. It was especially fascinating when younger and more experienced nurses shared stories about why they chose to begin a career in nursing. That allowed the newer nurses to hear a senior staffer's story, and it made the veteran nurses remember why they started nursing in the first place. Relationships were built, and extensions were made across disciplines and departments, and all were able to move forward with renewed mutual trust. The power of storytelling with an emphasis on identifying past actions that had borne good results provided the energy for everyone to imagine a better future.

I think that the most successful people (and groups) have a strong grasp of their own story. I really enjoy facilitating because it helps people use their story to take the actions they need to take. Helping others tell their story isn't just a useful business skill, it's a powerful bit of know-how across the board in life! For someone to share their story with you, they must trust you. And in order for them to trust you, you've got to ask the right questions in a spirit of sincere inquiry. Once you've opened a free discussion, you're more likely to change the way someone thinks, even if only slightly. That's wonderful, because thoughts lead to actions, and a slight shift of thinking can be the beginning of a big change in life.

* * * * *

"Leadership is the capacity to translate vision into reality." —*Warren Bennis*

Discussion Questions

Take action. Write down your responses. Share with a friend.

1. Describe a time when a stranger shared a story with you. How did it feel?

2. Write your short biography as if you were writing it five years from now. What does it say?

3. Have you ever made a little change that made a big difference? What did you do, and what was the effect?

4. Can you list ten ways that your thoughts influence your actions in your everyday life?

5. What's the best question that anyone has ever asked you? How did you answer?

6. What are you curious about? What actions can you take right now to learn more about it?

Stone Soup (Folktale)

There once was a traveler who came to a small village, weary from his long journey. He had nothing to eat, and hoped that somebody in the village would feed him, but as he went from door to door, each time the answer was no.

Undaunted, the traveler went to the village square, took a cooking pot from his bag, filled it with water, started a fire and dropped a single stone in the pot. A passing villager stopped and asked him what he was doing, and the traveler replied, "I'm making stone soup. Would you like to join me?" Intrigued, the villager asked if some carrots would be good in stone soup. "Sure," said the traveler. The villager brought carrots from his garden to add to the steaming water. Others brought potatoes, mushrooms, onions, salt, pepper, and corn, and all were tossed into the mixture. Finally, the traveler removed the stone from the pot and declared, "The stone soup is ready!" And, together they all enjoyed a hearty, delicious bowl of soup.

> **Moral:** We can accomplish more as individuals
> when we pool our resources and work together.

ACCEPT LOVE

"We need to learn to love ourselves first,
in all our glory and our imperfections." —John Lennon

It's that time again, time to look back and ahead. I feel truly grateful for the support I've received from friends and colleagues in the past; remember, receiving support is closely connected with also extending it in the spirit of service. I really do believe in the wisdom of bringing flowers, as much as I believe in the wisdom of receiving them with gratitude!

You can think of the Earl Graves, Sr. story as an example of "bringing flowers" (it's a bit strange, but I don't think he'd mind the comparison); certainly, it was an exciting experience for me to share a stage with him, but I was equally happy to share that experience with a lot of other lucky people! Support is an inherently mutual experience.

Once you've found a community of supportive people, things really start to heat up! You're free to be vulnerable and to take chances. You're also free to encourage other people's talents, accept other people's gifts and show them appreciation. The hard power of competition and drive has its place in life and in business; but the soft power of acceptance, vulnerability and asking for help is equally powerful.

By now, we've learned that being truly significant is really about getting better, little by little, day by day. But you can't always be in the driver's seat in life, and that's what the next stories are about.

13

Choosing to Share

"Every person in this life has something to teach me -- and as soon as I accept that, I open myself to truly listening." —Catherine Doucette

I often tell people that I've had the benefit of a luxurious life. Not the trust fund, jet-setting, haute-couture kind of luxury, but rather the luxury of choice. I've been fortunate to be able to focus on developing several businesses, and I have shaped my life according to my own vision.

When I was in my twenties and in the fray of running a business on a shoestring budget, often pulling long days and longer nights, I sometimes felt as if there wasn't time enough in the world and never would be. And yet, one day I chose to spend a lot of time on a project that had absolutely nothing to do with my business vision.

In those days I had an intern, Christine, who helped out with day-to-day tasks. Christine's mother had been a student of mine and we had developed a friendship, so that's how I met Christine.

After a promising start, suddenly Christine's energy on the job started to wane. She went from coming three days a week, to two days, and from two to one, until finally I became really concerned about her. I started calling her regularly to reassure her that she was a vital and valued part of my team. It was during one of these calls that Christine revealed to me that she was pregnant, and that her relationship was falling apart.

This new information put me in an awkward position because

Christine hadn't even told her own mother this news yet! Immediately, I started thinking about inviting Christine -- and her two other children -- to come and live with me! I could see that she needed stability, and that she didn't have too many options. But this obviously wasn't a simple decision for me. After all, three other people--and soon a newborn baby --living in my home with me would change my life completely. And, until then, my life had been completely under my control and on my schedule.

I told Christine to come.

Happily, as I offered this little family stability under my roof, I began to find my own balance, too, and in caring for them I received benefits, too. For example, before Christine and her family came to live with me, I wasn't eating breakfast regularly, but those three children needed a proper start to their day, so breakfast it was! Every single day. Likewise, Christine didn't have much money, so we worked to manage and pool our resources in the best way possible to keep food on the table for all five of us. We established routines, and I felt a new joy in being outwardly focused on the needs of others after years of going it solo.

I had lots of fun with the kids, and I was amazed to see how quickly my mothering instinct kicked in! We would take day trips to the zoo, or to go strawberry picking on a farm. I tried to expose them to things they might not have experienced without my influence, and I tried to share useful values and lessons that my parents had given to me -- simple things like saying "please" and "thank you." I felt like a big sister to Christine, too, as I helped her over this major bump in her road.

Previous to this, I had been focused solely on developing my business, with my eyes on a self-determined horizon. I was in complete control. But shifting gears to help cultivate a family that needed me, while a boon to them, was truly a gift to me. It brought nurturing back into my life, and the joy of giving and receiving love, which is the most luxurious reward there is.

Christine and I became trusting friends. And a long time after she had moved out on her own, now strengthened by the shelter I had provided to her little family, I would receive regular updates about her and the children. Our relationship has continued to be a source of joy to me over the years.

I learned that when you're on the course you've set for yourself, that's a great time to be a light for someone else who's trying to find her way, even if it involves re-organizing your schedule for a little while. Choosing to share with someone who needs what you have can throw you off-track for a little while, but it can also put you on exactly the right track as a human being.

* * * * *

"Good actions give strength to ourselves
and inspire good actions in others." —Plato

Discussion Questions

Take action. Write down your responses. Share with a friend.

1. For me, having choices is luxurious. What are the "luxuries" in your life?

2. When have you created choices for yourself?

3. What would you be willing to sacrifice or risk to help someone else?

4. Do you feel like you have enough choices available to you? List five ways you might act right now to create more.

5. What is your vision of your perfect life?

6. How you could use your perfect life to help others?

14

Walk With Me

"When nothing is sure, everything is possible." —Margaret Drabble

For those of us born with healthy bodies, learning to walk is a milestone that we don't remember. We take those first uncertain steps as vulnerable babies, someone takes a picture, and then we topple into the caring arms of an adult who is waiting to catch us. Once we get the hang of it, walking is no big deal! It's how we get from here to there, what we do on our way to more important things. Our body supports us, and we move forward, taking for granted the miracle of taking one, single step.

In April 2005, I was in the middle of an MBA program at Eastern University. One evening, though, while I was in my car in front of a local coffee shop, I got the alarming call from my doctor that the MRI I had taken recently was showing that I had breast cancer, and that the recommended treatment was a mastectomy. I'm a private person, but I decided two things sitting alone in that car: I wasn't going to let cancer derail me, and I wasn't going to go through it alone.

I stayed in my MBA program throughout the treatment, and after the mastectomy, I was told I needed to have chemotherapy. The thought of taking what is basically poison really scared me, and I knew I needed to strengthen both my mind and my body before undergoing the treatment. So I decided to take a walk, but not just any walk; I committed to the Susan G. Komen Walk for the Cure, a sixty mile walk over three days. Upon committing to do this marathon walk, I immediately felt stronger, because I was doing something while sick that most people wouldn't think of doing well! And besides the mental and physical preparation the walk offered, it was also a way for me to share my story with others. So I began telling people about my situation and my plan to complete the walk.

The outpouring of support was immediate. People sent notes and emails offering me words of comfort, and offering to sponsor my walk. At first, this response was completely overwhelming for me, but soon I felt a deep sense of gratitude for the many people who were reaching out to me with words of encouragement and love.

One of those people who reached outsurprised to me. I didn't know Susy very well when we were undergraduates at Princeton 25 years earlier, but when she learned about my cancer and my plan to complete the walk, she said she'd do it with me. And not only did she walk the whole sixty miles with me, she also flew from Minnesota to Philadelphia with *three other people* who walked in solidarity! Susy's support meant more to me than I can ever express.

Life had dealt me a severe blow, but I decided I would get up and walk again -- literally. And once I made that determination, Susy appeared as that smiling person with arms outstretched, saying, "keep on walking, baby, I've got you." The cancer treatment may have begun in the doctor's office, but the real healing began with this marathon walk and the support of Susy, her friends and the others who demonstrated solidarity with me.

No one learns to walk alone. No matter how old we are or what our circumstances, we always need other people to walk through life with us. Human contact, personal touch, and sincere connections are vital to our forward motion, and you may be surprised by the people who step up to the plate to help you -- when you have the courage to ask.

* * * * *

"Life is 10% what happens to me and 90% of how I react to it."
—John Maxwell

Discussion Questions

Take action. Write down your responses. Share with a friend.

1. Think of a time that you overcame a major challenge. How did you get yourself through it?

2. Think of a time that you were vulnerable and reached out to someone else for help. How did it feel?

3. Who is the person to whom you feel closest? Describe that relationship.

4. Describe a time when you needed to heal. How did you do it?

5. What relationships do you have that you think are helping you to meet your goals?

6. Which relationship(s) may not be helping you to meet your goals? What actions can you take right now to change those relationships?

15

Garden Groove

"Wisdom and penetration are the fruit of experience,
not the lessons of retirement and leisure." —Abigail Adams

When I was a little girl, my family kept a huge garden. Everyone had to pitch in, and the responsibility of weeding fell on my shoulders. At first, I found it annoying. I could see the point of it, but I couldn't see why *I* had to be the one to pull those green infiltrators out of the earth. It was just a burden! But slowly I began to fall in love with the whole process as I started to observe from close up the tiny seeds--bits of almost nothing-- grow into things that we could eat and that could support our lives. As I've grown older, I've never lost that early sense of the magic of helping things grow. Indeed, I've become more passionate about gardening as the years have passed, and it has taken on new layers of meaning for me over the years.

To start with, keeping a garden is sensually rewarding. It's a bounty for the senses! The feeling of my fingers in the soil, the smell of the earth after a rain, the scent of tomato and basil leaves, the sight of the delicate flowers of the cucumber and the heartier squash blossoms---all of these and more flood into me in one continuous stream of delight. I used to garden listening to music with headphones on, but later I began to appreciate the moment for what it was: profound yet simple, busy yet tranquil, and worthy of my full attention.

Once I learned to appreciate that experience, I started to notice parallels between everyday life and the activity of gardening. For me, the know-how involved in growing vegetables, flowers, and herbs is incredibly helpful in negotiating day-to-day life.

First of all, a good gardener is a great observer. Plants are living things that are part of a dynamic and fluid natural system, so it's important to play close attention to the little changes and to adjust accordingly. The process is much more than watering once a day and hoping for sunny weather! If you pay close attention to all the factors and do the hard work, things start to grow in your garden; the same is true in life. The more we provide the conditions for what we're trying to grow in correct balance and measure, the more positive outcomes we will reap.

Secondly, sharing what I harvest is an especially beautiful and useful aspect of gardening. One year, I walked around to my neighbors' homes, giving away baskets full of beautiful, home-grown cucumbers and squash. It's wonderful to see how much people appreciate something you grew or made yourself and then choose to share with them! The spirit and act of sharing has universal applications and brings unexpected rewards to both the giver and the receiver.

Still, I'm still absolutely fascinated with how weeds grow. Despite your best efforts, they pop up where you didn't plant them! Watching weeds is like watching action movies in slow motion –– they plot and plan and take root, as if the soil belongs to them. If ignored, weeds take over and choke out the plants you want to grow. As we've seen thus far in this book, even if you're careful and attentive to your garden, or the things that you're trying to grow in your life, weeds will still pop up–– in the form of unexpected challenges and obstacles.

You can see weeds as a nuisance as I did at first, or you can accept them as teachers, and as an integral part of the entire process with their own lessons to teach. Weeds are persistent! Weeds are opportunists! Weeds are incredibly successful, and they make do with very little encouragement. They are self-driven. How will you respond when weeds pop up in the garden of your life? You can choose to respond to weeds by giving up and letting your garden grow wild, or you can keep your hands in the earth and keep digging and paying close attention.

Focus on cultivating your garden, watching and listening to all the signs, until you get the harvest that *you* want.

*   *   *   *   *

"*Those who wish to sing, always find a song.*" —*Swedish Proverb*

Discussion Questions

Take action. Write down your responses. Share with a friend.

1. What are your hobbies? Do they teach you anything that you can apply to everyday life?

2. What do you feel you are currently "cultivating" in the garden of your life? Upon reflection, do you like the "crop" you are "cultivating"?

3. Is there something or someone who is like a "weed" in your life, but who might still have a lesson to teach you?

4. Describe a time when not paying attention cost you something. What happened?

5. What steps can you take to become a more patient person?

6. What activities make you feel calm and energized? Upon reflection, do you think you participate in those activities enough, and if not, why not?

The Ant and the Chrysalis (Aesop)

An Ant nimbly running about in the sunshine in search of food came across a Chrysalis that was very near its time of change. The Chrysalis moved its tail, and thus attracted the attention of the Ant, who then saw for the first time that it was alive. "Poor, pitiable animal!" cried the Ant disdainfully. "What a sad fate is yours! While I can run hither and thither at my pleasure and ascend the tallest tree, you lie imprisoned here in your shell, with power only to move a joint or two of your scaly tail." The Chrysalis heard all this, but did not try to make any reply.

A few days after, when the Ant passed that way again, nothing but the shell remained. Wondering what had become of its contents, he felt himself suddenly shaded and fanned by the gorgeous wings of a beautiful Butterfly. "Behold in me," said the Butterfly, "your much-pitied friend! Boast now of your powers to run and climb as long as you can get me to listen." So saying, the Butterfly rose in the air, and, borne along and aloft on the summer breeze, was soon lost to the sight of the Ant forever.

Moral: *Appearances are deceptive.*

BE SIGNIFICANT!

"You have everything you need to build something
far bigger than yourself." —Seth Godin

We're coming closer to the end of this book. You may have noticed by now how life often parallels itself, and puts us in situations as if to see if we've learned our lessons. I've faced multiple health challenges, but I chose not to let those define me. You may have faced life-changing challenges, too, and the same kinds of choices remain available to you. In fact, choice is one luxury with which most of us are born, but which many of us neglect. Like the ant in Aesop's tale, many people fail to recognize the butterfly in themselves and others; but when we know that we are significant, we can transform and achieve our full potential. We can choose to fly!

That's what it means to me to love life; it means to recognize that each of our choices is a kind of seed from which our future life will grow. It means paying attention to what's around us and working with it, because even when we're facing a garden full of weeds, we can still feel confident that we can cultivate a desirable crop. Throughout this book, I've encouraged you to consider your own story and your own choices. Ask yourself: What kind of life are you cultivating right now?

The stories in the following section are very simple. They're about the times that I've tried to take my appreciation for the gift of life, transform it into a force to create the best reality possible for myself and others and, by so doing, take flight and demonstrate my true significance.

16

Think: PSA

"It's your place in the world; it's your life. Go on and do all you can with it, and make it the life you want to live." —Mae Jemison

Experience is an expensive teacher. The benefit is that once you learn something through experience, you *really* know it. But the drawback is that experience can be a *slow* teacher. You poke here, you prod there, and eventually you find a solution. As a serial entrepreneur with over thirty years of business experience including seven positions at domestic and international corporations in four different industries, I've observed a pattern of behaviors in myself and others that I've systematized into three groups: passion-istas, seeker-istas, and action-istas.

Let me tell you about the "passion-istas" first. They're the "me first" type. They're the ones who absolutely, positively have to follow an idea because it's their passion. And that's great! Passion is powerful. But unless that passion is directed toward a real problem, unless there's a vision connecting that passion to a real-world purpose, it probably won't turn into anything. I know because I've been a passion-ista!

A number of years ago, fueled by a vision of a bountiful vegetable garden, I behaved like a classic passion-ista. I was steaming with a vision of months of home-grown, fresh vegetables, so no expense seemed unreasonable for my new outdoor container garden. I roamed the gardening section of my local big-box store with a flatbed cart and I eagerly filled it like an unsupervised child in a toy store. I bought a ton of stuff. Truth? I even ordered worm eggs. Yes, I did. I spent over $450 on gardening supplies in a single day!

But while I had a vision and the passion to go with it, I was missing a real plan and a process. I hadn't created garden layout, thought about who might care for my veggie paradise when I was away, nor had I made a budget! What's worse, after lifting all those 20-pound bags of soil multiple times and spending every dew-soaked morning in the garden, I had muscle pains and bug bites all over my body, and I was completely exhausted from getting up every day before sunrise to work in my "paradise"! Somehow, my passion had waned.

So I know from hard experience about being a "passion-ista"! True, passion is the spark, and there's great power in people who are so in love with something that they throw themselves at it with everything they've got. But balance is the key.

Which brings me to the second type of person. I'll call them the "seeker-istas". These are the people who are passionate, yet know they need help or more information, and actively look for it. They not only leave no stone unturned, they also dig beneath the stones! Quite often this type of person discovers useful information on their quest that transforms their passion into a focused concept.

After I decided that I wanted to pursue an MBA degree, I buried myself in research. I investigated 20 schools, and interviewed 10 alumni and current students of those institutions based on my connections. I attended open houses and talked to recruiters. I developed a matrix of the courses, tuition, and professors, practically re-writing the guide to MBA programs in the process! In some ways, my non-stop research was waste of time because in my zealousness to run everything through my own filter, I was blind to the value of resources that were already available. On the other hand, I did find exactly the right program for me. I was part of a community of adults learning and applying business know-how at the same time! I loved the people I met, and I couldn't wait for Thursday evenings to come so I could go to class!

The school search experience worked out; but my seeker-ista experiences haven't always ended well, and in my life journey there have also been plenty of times when I could have sought help and didn't. In 10th grade, I was two years younger than everyone else and I was sure I could get straight A's -- all by myself. It was, I suppose, a point of pride for me to succeed alone. One day, a kind teacher who knew I was struggling in Chemistry told me, "Frances, you've got to learn how to ask for help." Well, it took a while to learn that lesson, but now I know that while having the passion to seek out experiences is powerful, equally powerful is seeking out the support and information that will get you to the *best* results, quickly.

Finally, let's talk about the third type of person that I call the "action-ista". You've probably guessed already that these sort of people have passion, yes, but they are primarily about taking *action*. The action-ista is blessed with courage, but she can get into a lot of hot water by leaping before she looks! I have had numerous experiences as a business coach trying to repair the fallout after action-istas fail to seek before they leap! Some have signed long-term leases and sunk thousands of dollars into improvements like installing fixtures and knocking out walls, without first securing the approval of community boards, and licensing and inspection departments. The result? Financial loss, emotional distress, a tarnished reputation and damaged credit. Sometimes charging into battle is just what's needed, but it helps to have a plan first.

Many of the stories I share in this book are about my evolution as a person who blends these three personalities in a creative way. Remember my party planning business that I ran on a shoestring budget while I was in college? It was fueled by my passion for being curious, listening, and asking questions. And since I love to solve problems and connect the dots, I sought out ways to muster resources. I took action by posting flyers, finding out what would motivate a student to commit to working for me, and using cost analysis, logistics, marketing and payroll to create a business.

One thing I know for sure: no one goes it alone. Entrepreneurship is not a solo sport, and there are people along the way who will inform your journey and join your team. My passion for learning and sharing knowledge created opportunities for me to seek out people with similar interests, complementary skills, and proven experience. I've taken action. Of course not every situation has worked out as I dreamed. But today, as president of Significant Business Results LLC, I have an immensely rewarding career coaching entrepreneurs to achieve greater success in their businesses.

Any one of these entrepreneurial personalities I have discussed here can achieve goals, because each one is deeply engaged with life. But blended together, they are the surest route to success. It's about knowing yourself and what your default personality really is. Why? Because when you have this self-knowledge, you can find the complementary people that you need to achieve success. The caterpillar must spin its cocoon first in order tobecome the butterfly that takes flight!

How can you best remember the correct sequence? Think: PSA. No, not public service announcement, but rather Passion, then Seeking, and, finally, Action. Without this balance and order, you can easily become stuck in any venture that you embark upon. However, by obeying the natural order and surrounding yourself with people who complement your strengths, you will turn into the butterfly you dream yourself to be!

* * * * *

"Do what you can, where you are, with what you have." — Teddy Roosevelt

Discussion Questions

Take action. Write down your responses. Share with a friend.

1. Think of a time you were passionate about something. What was it, and what happened?

2. Think of a time you sought out a person or service to complement your strengths. What happened?

3. Think of a time you took action on something you were passionate about. Did it work out? What happened?

4. What are you most passionate about right now?

5. What or who do you need to seek out to help activate your passion?

6. Can you list three specific actions that you can take right now to turn your passion into an enterprise?

7. Upon reflection, which personality (passion-ista, seeker-ista, action-ista) do you think is your "default"? Explain in detail.

17

Bringing Up (My) Baby

*"Loving a baby is a circular business, a kind of feedback loop.
The more you give the more you get and the more you get
the more you feel like giving." —Penelope Leach*

All of us live in three worlds at once: the world of the self, the world of the family, and the world of the community. Depending on a person's priorities, the focus may lie with one or all of these worlds at any given time. This matters because what someone is committed to determines where she will focus her passion, her care, and her energy.

Throughout my life and career, I've made decisions driven by my passion for creating great businesses, and I've developed a deep sense of commitment, informed by my early family experiences, especially those with my mother.

My mother worked hard to nurture me and my sisters and provide us with the best life could offer. Her idea of nurturing included ensuring that we had a good education, and clarifying what was expected of us by both our family and our community. That way, we understood "the rules", we could anticipate the outcomes of our actions, and learn to make wise decisions.

Both my mother and father were pioneers, because both went to medical school at a time when there were few blacks doing so. This took tremendous courage and self-discipline on their part. And when our family moved to the suburbs in the 1970s, even though I was very young, I perceived that both of my parents feared some backlash because they were black and joining a middle-class suburban community where few black families had settled. Even as a very young girl, I recall having some floating anxiety about burning crosses and the physical safety of my family; so when the welcoming committee did come to the door of the new house, I sat quietly at the top of the stairs wondering if my mother was hesitating to open the door because she shared my unspoken anxiety. But despite this undercurrent of social "otherness", our mother always went out of her way to make sure that we children knew that our safety and our personal and intellectual development were her highest priorities; and, as a result, my sisters and I grew up with a sense of security and well-being.

I have carried forward my mother's profound sense of personal responsibility into my professional life; I've always felt that in a 24-hour day, I'll take as much time as needed to do my best to protect and nurture my business. So while some people seek to become musical virtuosos, intellectual authorities, or stellar spouses or parents, I have always sought to become the best business person I could be, and my business has always received from me the same loving care that my mother gave to me and my sisters. But unlike my mother, I didn't choose the path of having children, although it is certainly possible to do so and still have a successful business career! That said, for me fulfillment has come primarily from developing a healthy business, and it has always required from me the same sense of discipline, direction, courage, clarity and, yes, love that a child receives from a mother. My business is my baby.

Warren Buffet famously said, "You can't produce a baby in one month by getting nine women pregnant." That's another way of saying that, like children, businesses take time to grow and they go through pre-determined stages. My "business baby" has had to have vaccinations (business plans), doctor visits (to the accountant, lawyer, insurance agent, and banker), and schooling (at Business School, or with a business coach). And as a "business parent", I've endured sleepless nights wondering where my next client or line of credit was going to come from so that I could feed my "baby". Furthermore, as with a child, the way you care for a business in the first few years of its life will determine whether it thrives and grows or not. And once, I nearly lost my "baby".

Remember my contract with the City of Pittsburgh to train city employees in software skills? Well, the terms I had agreed to specified that I would provide the service first, and get paid 120 days later, which is not unusual for City contracts. With a payroll of $500 a week and approximately six weeks before the first money would come in, that meant having a minimum of $8,000 in reserve, plus a $2,000 tax buffer! Add on rent, utilities, classroom supplies, paper for the printer, books for the students, and the truth was that I really needed an additional $10,000 in reserve. If you do the math, you'll see that adds up to a $20,000 reserve!

From the start, I knew the money would be tight. But it got even tighter when the City's check didn't show up on time! No check, no electric bill and no payroll. No payroll, no employees, and no trainings! No trainings, no business. My "business baby" was going to starve to death if I didn't do something -- and fast. Unfortunately, I didn't have a good working relationship with a bank so that I could secure a line of credit or a loan. And while I made a list of all the things I owned that I could possibly sell for cash, it turned out to be a disappointingly short list. In desperation, went to my parents to ask if they could float me a short-term loan, and they said no. "It was your decision to go into this business", my mother explained, "now you have to deal with it." Embarrassed, I went to my employees and warned them that I might not be able to make the next payroll. Things were looking pretty bleak.

Determined to save my business, I decided to create a new plan in which I detailed how I would manage company finances going forward. I made weekly, monthly and quarterly projections that compared revenue to expenses. I presented this new plan to my parents, identified the funds to pay them back, and they graciously loaned me the money. I made payroll (barely), but I had suffered having had to admit how shaky things had looked, to people who were counting on me, and had children (real, live children) at home to feed. I was ashamed, frustrated and infuriated with myself because I had put my "baby", and other people in jeopardy.

Thank heavens for all of us, my "business baby" survived! But a lot of businesses don't survive beyond the first 5 years. According to the U.S. Small Business Administration, over 50% of small businesses fail in the first five years from a variety of causes including lack of experience (check), poor credit arrangements (check), insufficient capital (check), and a variety of other good (and predictable) reasons. But I learned my lessons, and I made moves to give my "business baby" a safe place in which to grow up. I had sustained a few bruises to my ego, but I found out that I was not alone; and perhaps most importantly, I found out that I was ready to do whatever it took to ensure that my business not only survived, but thrived.

There are growing pains that come with starting a business. But each time I did it, I learned, developed more tools, and things got just a little bit easier. Ultimately, choosing what you want to nurture in life is a personal decision, but whether it's a "business baby", a child or something else, it is imperative to create a secure place for it to grow. It's wonderful that each of us has the power to choose, and to give life everything she's got.

* * * * *

"A wise man will make more opportunities than he finds."
—*Sir Francis Bacon*

Discussion Questions

Take action. Write down your responses. Share with a friend.

1. What do you nurture in your life? Why have you made this choice?

2. When have you failed to provide a secure environment for something you love to thrive? What happened?

3. How can you create a more secure environment right now to nurture what matters most to you?

4. What are your top three priorities in life?

5. How can you do a better job of respecting those priorities?

6. If you had a magic wand and could change one thing in the world, what would it be? Why?

18

Can You Hear Me Now?

*"The most common way people give up their power
is by thinking they don't have any." —Alice Walker*

Earlier in my business career, I would speak up in a meeting to suggest an idea and then get no response––as if what I said had not been heard by anyone at all. Then often later, someone else would make the same exact suggestion and be met with resounding approval –– especially if that someone else happened to be a man! The first time it happened, I took a moment to check in with myself. Was I being too sensitive? Was I making it up? After it happened on multiple occasions, I knew that I wasn't imagining things.

I call the phenomenon of speaking up, being ignored, and having your idea poached, the "can you hear me now" effect. Corporate America has made some progress in this regard, but it has a long way to go, and to this day women and people of color face challenges in the workplace that others just don't have to think about. I've shared this one example, but there are many. I am sure that my gender, my ethnicity and probably my young age were a part of the reason that people back then didn't "hear" me.

But I believe that my experience of not being heard was also connected to something even more basic: power and perception. Initially, I felt shocked and stifled when people didn't pay attention to me. I had a track record of quality work and excellent performance, I knew that my ideas were valuable, and I was able to demonstrate that value. But in that particular context, people didn't *perceive* me as a leader, despite the image I had of myself. And if power is anything, it's a game of perception. I quickly learned the value of understanding and participating in team dynamics. So I started to attend the "meeting before the meeting," the brief informal pow-wow where people got together as peers before the formal theater of The Meeting. I'd share my ideas there, and when they came up in the context of The Meeting, I'd second them and in that way I was able at least to make my ideas and myself at little more heard.

This strategy worked well to validate others and to make them feel comfortable around me, but it wasn't a plan that made me entirely happy. I hadn't successfully shifted the power balance, I had only modulated its effects on me and others. In hindsight, I realize that I could have sought out peers in similar positions at other companies so that we could have supported each other, developed more strategies, and reported back to each other on our progress. I could have networked.

Apart from perception, another big part of power is preparation. That includes hard skills like taking notes in meetings and using them in later conversations, or developing sharp negotiating techniques. But it also includes consciously developing a feeling of well-being and confidence by deliberately participating in communities and networks of people that appreciate, encourage, and reward your talent and performance. Today, there are plenty of resources like leanin.org that create this atmosphere, and provide an almost "ready-made" community for women in business. When I started out, networking this way was a lot more difficult!

Eventually, I decided the "battle of influence" wasn't worth fighting –– not in the corporate context, where the rules were made by someone else and subject to change without warning. I started seeking out arenas outside of the workplace, often as an entrepreneur, where I could excel, be valued for my voice and my ideas, and where I got paid well for speaking up! By consistently putting myself in situations where I was valued and compensated, I built my own business and, more importantly, I created a circle of influence that reached far beyond a single boardroom.

As a business coach, I now work with entrepreneurs who are positioned to challenge the exclusive elite power structure that stifles and restricts anyone who's not a member of the "in" club. Together, we continue to create our own inclusive power structure, and our own dynamic influence in the world. We continue to shape the business landscape, respond to each other, and reward ourselves. And as we succeed in our individual fields of endeavor, we keep asking those whose aim is to keep a tight grasp on power, "Can you hear me now?"

* * * * *

"Don't worry when you are not recognized,
but strive to be worthy of recognition." —Abraham Lincoln

Discussion Questions

Take action. Write down your responses. Share with a friend.

1. What does power mean to you?

2. What kind of power do you feel you possess?

3. Describe a time when you felt like an outsider. What specifically did other people do to make you feel that way? How did you respond?

4. When do you feel most confident? Least confident?

5. Think of a situation in which you felt (or feel) weak, ineffective or completely powerless. Who could help you achieve greater power? What strategies might you employ?

19

The Invisible Woman

"The most basic and powerful way to connect to another person is to listen. Just listen. Perhaps the most important thing we ever give each other is our attention." —Rachel Naomi Remen

In the last chapter, we talked about how not being perceived as part of the "in" group can be a frustrating experience, even if you find ways to manage the resistance and get in your two cents. For many of us who have been perceived as "outsiders" by those in power, the best route has been to actively develop our own support networks and find validation outside of the traditional power structure. After all, just because the ants around you can't see that you're a butterfly doesn't mean you aren't one! But you may have to first go through a few difficult experiences to earn your wings and prove to others – as well as to yourself – that you can really fly.

Developing strategies to get your ideas heard by others who are higher up in the organizational food chain is important. But what about the flip side of that coin? What about learning to wield your own power strategically, and to be conscious of the sometimes intimidating effect you may have on others? Acknowledging your power and simultaneously being sensitive to the effect it has on other people is a very important lesson to learn; because in this life it's not just being acknowledged that counts, it's also leaning in to really listen other people.

Business coaches like me are professional listeners and observers, sounding boards who help entrepreneurs see what they sense, hear what they say, and pay close attention to what their gut is telling them. What I do takes a lot of training and skill, and my professional fees are equal to those of a lawyer or accountant. Why am I sharing this with you? Because I want to emphasize that like lawyers and accountants, and given my demanding schedule I have limited time to volunteer my professional services. But now I will tell you about how one time I extended my hand to help someone, and got it bitten in the process!

In my work as an adjunct university professor, I bring guest speakers to my classes, encourage my students to pursue their entrepreneurial dreams, and hold them accountable for taking significant action. One of these students was a bright young woman, and when she sought my advice about whether her non-profit organization idea had "legs" or not, I was interested. Her passion was to create an organization to help empower women to believe in themselves, stand up, negotiate, and be substantially recognized for their contributions. Because her dream was something that I also believed in, I decided to volunteer as a consultant to help her develop her concept and achieve her organizational mission the way she envisioned it. She was thrilled to have me on board.

Fast forward a few months, and I was volunteering many hours in planning sessions, email communications, providing advice and experience, creating databases, and suggesting ways to measure results. I even traveled from Philadelphia to New York City to support her first volunteer event, and I felt happy to do it. She felt happy, too, because her project was moving from dream to reality, and even gaining international exposure!

As we talked about next steps, I began to share how I'd like to see my role shift from a volunteer to a paid consultant as her organization grew. I suggested potential scenarios on how we might rearrange our roles to focus on our individual strengths, and how we could create a fee structure that I could live with. After all, as a keynote speaker who regularly earns up to $10,000 for a presentation, I was familiar with the process! And while I realized that we weren't yet at the stage to make fees like that possible, I felt comfortable being authentic and forthright with her.

This is where the disconnect happened, though I did not see it at the time. I was talking about a project with all the usual professional requirements, deliverables, and fees; but she could only see that her "baby" was still young, and the idea of aggressively pursuing fee-based projects like I was suggesting felt too "business-ey" and threatening to her. We were not on the same page.

But, like a bull in a china shop, I keep charging forward! I saw more clients, more revenues, more profits, and with my thick skin, sharp horns and head to the ground, I didn't see how terrified she was at the sound of my onrushing hoofs! I pressed on, even as her emails to me began to change in tone and content. Then one day, she phoned me to say that the time had come for us to "clarify our roles" relative to the organization and, while I agreed that clarification was a good idea, I *still* wasn't getting the message! I know now that this was her veiled way of asking me to back off, because even though my ideas were good ones and came from years of success in the corporate arena, she felt overpowered by me and my ideas. She stopped soliciting advice, instead submitting curt requests for quotes. Things were getting weird. But when I expressed my concern at this change of tone, she fell silent.

Finally, this uncomfortable situation took a decisive turn. I received a last-minute invitation to a high-profile volunteer event for her organization, which I attended. The event was phenomenal, well-organized and truly a testament to the talented organizer that she had become. I was part of an invite-only photo op at the event. But when the photo was published, to my complete astonishment I had been carefully Photoshopped out of the image! I had become the Invisible Woman.

For me, that was the last straw. I was furious at being treated in this inconsiderate, passive-aggressive way after all my efforts to bring clarity, focus and structure to her work. After all, people pay me good money to do what I had been doing for her for free! How dare she treat me that way! Like the wolf in the story of the three little pigs, I was ready to huff and to puff and the blow the whole house down. But upon reflection, I realized something very, very important: This wasn't a house made of sticks, or straw or even bricks. In fact, *it wasn't my house at all!* In my enthusiasm to bring my business ethic to *her* project, I hadn't respected the central fact that it was her organization to run as she pleased. I hadn't been listening carefully enough to the various subtle, and eventually not-so-subtle, ways in which she had been trying to ask me to stop overpowering her.

As I had failed in "hearing" her, she too had failed to be direct with me and tell me that she needed space so that she could assume her rightful spot at the center of her project. But not everyone is able to face conflict head-on, and few people enjoy it. I've found in my life that difficult conversations don't get better as they age; and like dust balls or mold, conflicts get bigger the longer you avoid dealing with them. My conflict with a fellow entrepreneur was a perfect example of this.

You know by now that I learn a lot from my garden, so let me share a garden lesson with you now. Some people like to buy their tomato plants pre-sprouted in pots, but I like to start them from seed so that I can observe the whole cycle, from a dry seed to a flourishing plant that produces delicious, juicy tomatoes. When you start tomatoes from seed, you have to incubate them under hot grow-lights to get those seeds to wake up. Then one day tiny cotyledons, those all-important first embryonic leaves of the new plant, are popping their little heads out of the soil. Those first leaves are drawing stored energy both from the seed itself and from the new energy of the hot light above them. But once the little plants develop true leaves that can photosynthesize, you must move them away from the hot grow-lights, because if you don't, the plant won't develop a strong stem of its own. No juicy tomatoes.

At a certain stage in her development as a leader, my fellow entrepreneur must have felt that in order to grow her own "stem", she needed to distance herself from me, the "hot light". Would I have preferred it if she had talked to me directly instead of just erasing me from a group photograph? Absolutely! But I had make a mistake by not hearing her indirect calls for help – so she made me "disappear"! It's a good idea to learn to be sensitive to what other people really want and to the language they use to express those wants: if you don't, you run the risk of your contribution being undervalued; and in these days of social media, conflicts can become digitally amplified extremely quickly!

Becoming the "invisible woman" was a very painful learning experience for me. However, I was ultimately able to help a fellow entrepreneur clarify her own leadership role within her organization, establish boundaries, and learn to make decisions about the kind of support she wanted and who she wanted to get it from. And I learned that in one's efforts to be heard, it's always a good idea to remember how to listen.

* * * * *

"Courage is what it takes to stand up and speak;
courage is also what it takes to sit down and listen." —*Winston Churchill*

Discussion Questions

Take action. Write down your responses. Share with a friend.

1. Describe a time when you were a good listener. What happened? How were you effective as a listener? What feedback did you receive to validate that you were a good listener?

2. Describe a time when you missed cues that led to miscommunication, threatening a relationship. How did you miss the cues? What lessons did you learn from that situation?

3. When have you received a message indirectly? Why do you think the message was delivered indirectly? How do you know you interpreted the message correctly or incorrectly?

4. When have you delivered a message to someone else indirectly? Was there a reason you chose to be indirect? Do you think in retrospect that it was a good decision or a bad one, and why?

5. Describe a time when you felt as if another person was making you feel "invisible". What did you do about it?

6. What could you do right now to listen better to other people?

20

Tea, Anyone?

"You can't use up creativity. The more you use,
the more you have." —Maya Angelou

Sometimes, simplicity is the seed of the sublime. I've learned to appreciate the ordinary things in life because there was a time when I had to do without them. For a brief period, I was unable to choose where I went or when, or what clothes I would wear. I was even deprived of the small pleasure of tying my shoes.

After I had a paralyzing stroke, I had to work hard to finally regain some freedom of movement, but that was only the beginning. I still had to attend physical therapy, which is a notoriously challenging and potentially dispiriting process. But early on in my recovery, I determined that I would take ownership of the experience.

When doctors came, I extended my hand, introduced myself, and asked plenty of questions. Many looked surprised. "Wait a minute," they seemed to think, "you're the patient, and we're supposed to be asking you the questions!"

But I looked at it this way: first, they were learning from me during the course of the treatment, so it was reasonable that I could also learn from them. And second, since I was living on the ward, I would treat it as my home, and that meant engaging the people with whom I was sharing the space in a direct and active way. My approach to recovery was to believe that my personhood -- that is, my mind, my will, my charisma, and my strength -- wasn't paralyzed, even if my body was. With that attitude, it was much easier to remain fully engaged and to really pay attention to my body during the recovery process. Though it was difficult to re-learn basic movements that I had once taken for granted, I made quick progress. And soon, it was nearly time to leave the ward.

Before the stroke, I had been having regular tea dates with the group of my friends I've already told you about. Well, they decided that we should have a tea date right there at the hospital! Since I had been sharing my life with a group of fellow patients for a month, I thought it would only be right to organize something that included *everyone* on the floor. So I mentioned the idea to the nurses and they were excited to help! There was a computer that I could use to plan the party, too, and I remember one of the nurses quipping, "If you're well enough to use that computer, it might be time for you to go."

She may have been right, but in a way, organizing that tea party was as important a part of my recovery as the daily physical therapy was. It was a signal that I was returning in spirit to my everyday life, as well as in body. I was returning to *myself*. It was a passage. And it was even more significant because I was able to share that passage with all the people around me.

Therapy, like many other experiences, is only as helpful as you let it be. The mental and the physical are intimately interconnected. Now, I wasn't planning a "healing" event; it was really just a simple tea party! But the benefits were clear. And quickly, the nurses realized how organizing this kind of collective experience had generated a feeling of community and a renewed energy to the routine on the ward. So, replicating our tea party experience, two weeks later the nurses organized a Super Bowl party! As far as I know, such events are now part of life on the ward.

There was one especially delicious aspect of the tea party in the hospital. I had been planning to use disposable plates and utensils, but when I shared that with one of the nurses, she offered some lovely, real china that had been stored away, unused for a long time. So, needless to say, we used that instead, and what a perfect highlight it was! I had entered the hospital unable to tie my own shoes, but I left it drinking tea from fine china with my fellow physical therapy patients! It was a rich and memorable way to transition back from dependent patient to empowered person.

Instead of a succumbing to a bleak and depressing experience, I accepted my circumstances and consciously stayed positive and active -- on my terms. No matter what situation you are in, the simple step of taking ownership of your experience can lead to surprisingly wonderful outcomes.

* * * * *

"Whatever the mind of man can conceive and believe, it can achieve."
—*Napoleon Hill*

Discussion Questions

Take action. Write down your responses. Share with a friend.

1. What does it mean to you to be "at home?"

2. Describe a time when you shared a positive experience with a lot of people. What happened and how did it feel?

3. Describe a time when you took ownership of an experience that most people would see as negative or defeating. What happened and how did it feel?

4. Have you ever supported someone who was ill? How did you help? How did it feel to help?

5. What was the last thing you celebrated?

6. What have you not celebrated, now or in the past, that you would like to celebrate? How would you do it?

A FINAL WORD

It has been a joy to share my stories with you. I've woven in and out of events and the times, places and people of my life, and while it may not be the most linear way to tell a story, it is definitely closer to how things really happen! Real life doesn't come in neatly packaged boxes, and that's exactly why it's so important for us to collect and organize our stories, and examine them closely for their meaning so that we can use them as guides for what's to come.

I trust that by answering the questions after each chapter you've begun to make inroads into shaping your own personal vision. Remember that your story is ongoing! I challenge you to revisit the discussion questions many times by yourself or in a group, and to write down your answers to them anew each time to uncover fresh insights from the always-unfolding story of your life. As you continue to investigate yourself and your motivations, you will be surprised to see differences between your first responses and your new ones. When you look at your first answers later, it may seem as if someone familiar to you, perhaps a cousin or confidante, initially answered the questions rather than you, yourself! Resist the temptation to judge your early responses in any way, and simply know that even from this very moment, you will surely grow, and your views, beliefs and wisdom will mature with you. And that's a good thing.

Part of being significant is to always measure yourself and your choices against these key questions:

▶ Am I telling my own authentic story?

- ▶ Am I living in line with my values?
- ▶ Am I being respectful?
- ▶ Am I being respected?
- ▶ Am I recognizing opportunities?
- ▶ Am I making my own, authentic choices?
- ▶ Am I making pragmatic choices?
- ▶ Am I taking positive steps?
- ▶ Am I finding allies?
- ▶ Am I learning to lead?
- ▶ Am I loving the person I am?
- ▶ Am I loving the person I'm becoming?
- ▶ Am I being significant?

As you progress in your journey, you will remove the question marks from this list, and the questions will become affirmations. That's how you'll know that you're on your way! Asking good questions is the key to eliciting useful answers, and that's why you will revisit these questions over and over again. These questions and your answers to them are like the pencil marks on a door-frame that a parent uses to mark a child's growth; and you are parenting yourself, you are in charge of charting your own growth and making sure that you are doing what you need to do to rise to the heights that you dream of reaching.

Significant people understand that the only constant is change. They seek out change in ways that are healthy and that create dynamic, exciting circumstances and relationships for themselves and others. You are a significant person! No matter what actions you take or mistakes you make along the way, at your core is a powerful and creative person; inside the unpolished stone is a sparkling gem.

If there's one thing that I want you to take away from this book, it's this: you are creating your story and living it simultaneously. You may never find yourself in a boardroom, and you may never create community over a cup of tea. You may never have your authority questioned by a drunk person, or take a whole family that desperately needs you into your home. I certainly hope you are fortunate enough not to be struck down by a stroke or cancer, and maybe it isn't even your dream as it was mine to run a successful business! But the details of each person's story are not as important as the recognition that *no matter what your circumstances,* you have within you all the available energy, conditions and experiences you need to start transforming yourself and your situation. The seed of success is within you. Right here, right now.

If you're a new college graduate looking for your first job, an entrepreneur, a working mother, a non-profit organizer, or if you're starting or re-starting a career later in life, you can take your own stories, organize them, and use them to create opportunity. *You* are the only one who can tend *your* garden, and keeping your garden weed-free is a daily activity. Once you notice an opportunity or feel a passion that you think you must explore further, that's when you bring to bear all the tools you've acquired in your life -- and perhaps a few that you've learned from this book! -- to catch that glimmer of something good and transform it into something great.

You are already significant, simply because you are awake and participating in the marvelous experience of life. Living is a privilege, so honor that privilege. Take chances, be vulnerable, find allies and build on opportunities. Give with your heart, allow yourself to receive help when you need it, admit your mistakes and then correct them. Be creative. Be yourself.

Significantly yours in success,
Franne McNeal, MBA

About the Author

Franne McNeal, MBA, is the woman's voice for branding, business strategy and bold personal leadership success. Called the "significant business results coach," Franne helps her clients focus their energy to take action and achieve increased confidence, clarity and clout! She is the author of the book *Significant! From Frustrated to FranneTastic*, the women's storybook of "mining your mind for what matters".

As a breast cancer conqueror and stroke survivor, Franne shares stories of her own tenacity and prowess to help thousands of women discover their own strengths, monetize their passions, and add value to their communities. Franne is committed to integrating people, process and performance and to helping women achieve a dynamic understanding of how to "lean in", focus their energy for action and step up to significance in their business and personal lives.

Franne has had a remarkable career in sales, marketing and training within Fortune 500 corporations. In addition, she is a university professor, an author, a serial entrepreneur, and an award-winning business coach. Franne's keen insights have helped her clients generate millions in revenue, increase sales, improve cash flow, reduce expenses and expand profitability. Franne's motivational keynote speeches about achieving Significant Business Results have been well-received by hundreds of groups, from professional associations and universities, to entrepreneurial and corporate audiences. She is a regular contributor to print and online publications, including Black Enterprise and Lean In.

Franne McNeal earned a BA from Princeton University, and a MBA from Eastern University. She was recognized with Eastern University's Perseverance Award (2007) and was named one of the 100 Most Influential Black Women in Philadelphia by the NAACP in 2008, and honored as a Woman of Distinction by Main Line Today Magazine in 2014. Franne McNeal lives in the Philadelphia, PA area.

SIGNIFICANT! COMMUNITY

Connect! Would you like to connect with Franne McNeal and the Significant! community as you chart your own uniquely significant journey?

Register free at **www.SignificantYou.com**. There, you will be able to:

▶ Connect with like-minded people
▶ Access useful resources
▶ Download additional tools
▶ Participate in live virtual events
▶ Organize and attend local and regional events
▶ Share your Significant! stories
▶ Meet Franne McNeal

If you would like to interview Franne McNeal, invite her to be a keynote speaker, provide an executive workshop, engage her participation in a panel discussion, or involve her in your next online or international event, please reach out to her at **Media@SignificantYou.com**.

CPSIA information can be obtained at www.ICGtesting.com
Printed in the USA
BVOW04s1248140516

447784BV00005B/9/P

9 780979 164361